TO FOOL A GLASS EYE

TO FOOL A GLASS EYE

Camouflage versus Photoreconnaissance in World War II

ROY M. STANLEY II

Smithsonian Institution Press
Washington, D.C.

Dedication

With great love and affection, this book is dedicated
to my mother, Pauline Becker Stanley. She was the
first to teach me about colour, shapes, textures and
tones. She also gave me my first lesson in camouflage
– with a meatloaf.

Published 1998 in the United States of America
by Smithsonian Institution Press.

ISBN 1-56098-568-2

Library of Congress Catalog Number is 98-84486

First published in the United Kingdom in 1998
by Airlife Publishing Ltd., Shrewsbury.

Typeset by Phoenix Typesetting, Ilkley, West Yorkshire.
Printed in England by Butler and Tanner Ltd., Frome and London,
not at government expense.

04 03 02 01 00 99 88   5 4 3 2 1

PREFACE

In this age of multi-sensor, long-duration reconnaissance, camouflage is almost passé, except in a purely tactical context. It wasn't so fifty years ago. In the 1940s, aerial reconnaissance flights were of short duration and the only tools against camouflage were aerial photography and visual observation. Worse yet, a reconnaissance mission could only cover a small section of enemy territory with cameras holding just enough film for 200–250 exposures. In this environment, camouflage seemed to have potential to protect people, places and things a belligerent considered particularly valuable or vulnerable.

World War I-based conventional wisdom said that camouflage could be effective against observation and attack. The camoufleur's natural enemy, the aerial photo interpreter, had as his weapons the knowledge that there are no straight lines in nature, an understanding of what various human activities looked like on the face of the earth, a good memory, and a highly developed suspicion that if something didn't look right, it probably wasn't.

Photo interpreters (PIs) sought to not only identify industrial complexes by type but also to discover what was being produced and how much, thus adding to an understanding of war-making potential. This was particularly true for industries making primary war equipment (planes, tanks, submarines, etc.). Camouflage was frequently used to deny specific production knowledge when the existence of the factory could not be concealed. In similar fashion, if a military installation or assemblage couldn't be completely disguised, the number and type of equipment present might be. Ferreting out detailed knowledge of military hardware in a given area could disclose enemy intentions, or at the very least,

capabilities, so camouflage was used to cloud or distort the picture and the PI learned to penetrate it.

The subject of camouflage has been covered in many books since World War I and it isn't my purpose to retell a well-told tale. Those other works documented the history and theory of camouflage or went into elaborate detail on the various camouflage patterns for specific equipment. Some went on to address the success or failure of various famous concealment or deception efforts as they relate to specific military operations. But, all of those earlier books approached the subject of camouflage from the viewpoint of the people making the camouflage – the side working to deceive. That only gives half of the story.

These chapters attempt to show the other side of the contest – camouflage as viewed from the perspective of military intelligence personnel or attacking forces trying to discover and penetrate it. I also provide photographic examples of camouflage that earlier books on WW II described but didn't show. Where possible, aerial photographs are used to illustrate points because they were the primary means by which camouflage was uncovered and are closest to the aircrew's viewpoint: the view a warring party most sought to disrupt.

While researching this book, I relied upon help from a number of people at the National Archives, the Defense Intelligence Agency and the Pentagon's Army Library, especially Mr Paul LaBar, the best boss I ever had. In producing the book, I owe thanks to Mr A. D. R. Simpson and Peter Coles of Airlife Publishing. Most significant of all were my wife, Mary Ellen, and son, Roy (Capt. USAFR). Without their support and encouragement this book would not have reached printing. Thank you all.

Note on Photographs

Except as noted in the photo credits, the aerial and ground photographs presented in this book were originally collected for intelligence purposes during WW II and came from intelligence archives. Most, if not all of them have been transferred to the National Archives Still or Aerial Photo Libraries. They have been oriented for viewing in the book to portray how a photo interpreter or intelligence analyst would look at them. Ground photo orientation is obvious. Obliques are shown as they would be seen from the collection aircraft. Verticals are arranged so the shadows fall toward the viewer (i.e. the bottom of the page). This usually puts north somewhere between the bottom left and bottom right corners of the photo. To have shadows falling away from the viewer gives the impression of reversing hills and gullies.

Some of the photos still carry security markings, but none of them are actually classified any longer. *RESTRICTED* is no longer recognised as a classification, and by 1975 all of the *CONFIDENTIAL* and *SECRET* photos included here had been downgraded by the Department of Defense or the Archivist of the United States (based upon 30 years passing since the events photographed).

All the annotations, except arrows like this ➡ or this ➡ were put on these photos between 1939 and 1945 by intelligence personnel. Those other arrows are mine, and are the only changes made to the imagery since it was used in the war. In many cases, particularly the aerials, you are seeing what World War II intelligence specialists saw and used in their analysis or for operational activities such as crew briefings.

CONTENTS

(1-1) German photo of Moscow, 22 July 1941. Red Square and other open spaces around the Kremlin were camouflaged with painted buildings in an attempt to make this critical centre blend into the surrounding blocks of buildings. German annotations indicate damage from a bombing raid.

Opponents in the Great Game

An Introduction to Camouflage and Photo Intelligence

Morning shadows were still long in Moscow streets on 22 July 1941 and Luftwaffe aircraft were already overhead. The Soviet capital had first been struck ten days earlier, and on several days since. German bombers hit the city again on 21 July and the plane overhead this time was a twin-engined Luftwaffe photo-reconnaissance aircraft sent to document the latest damage. Soviet fighters and anti-aircraft were powerless to stop the high flying German reconnaissance plane – they couldn't reach its altitude.

Driven by necessity, in 30 days of war the Soviets had already proven themselves masters of tactical camouflage. It was only natural that they would try to camouflage the most central parts of this most central of governments. High above Moscow, the German aircrew may have had a little trouble picking out Red Square, but they knew exactly where it was from the nearby bend in the Moscow River. The reconnaissance pilot knew that Luftwaffe Intelligence technicians would have no trouble in locating the Kremlin, or nearby bomb damage, on the crisp black-and-white imagery he would deliver.

Three hours later, in a Luftwaffe cantonment miles behind the eastward rushing front lines, film from the plane's two huge aerial cameras was quickly processed. The two long rolls of negative film, each with 180 individual exposures, were mounted on glass-fronted light tables. Photo interpreters (PIs) began the task of plotting the area covered and minutely examining every part of every one of the nearly foot square negatives.[1] When they got to the frames covering Moscow, it is easy to imagine the German PIs grinning. Camouflage painting to simulate buildings on the bricks in Red Square could not have been designed or executed by anyone who had ever been up in an aeroplane (photo 1-1).

This vignette introduces the antagonists who feature in the rest of this book. On one side were the people on the ground – the camouflagers (some called them camoufleurs). Their objective was to protect key assets by hiding a force or factory, deceiving an enemy as to what was hidden, or confusing an attacker just long enough to cause some weapons to miss. Their means were paint, covering nets, constructing false-works and dummies or decoys.

On the other side were the aerial photo-reconnaissance flights (usually) high overhead, and the eyes of photo interpreters straining to penetrate the various camouflage and deception efforts. Their purpose was to locate, analyse minutely and identify installations and equipment the enemy thought important enough to hide. By prying out the secrets hidden underneath camouflage, these technicians were the first important step leading to the destruction of something an enemy thought significant.

Since it is usually applied only to the most valuable things, the paradox of camouflage is that if it works it protects, but, if it fails it tells an enemy who can penetrate the camouflage just what the other side values most – thereby making a pointer for attack.

Each of the World War II belligerents had experts working on both sides of the deadly camouflage game, but they did not all play with the same degree of finesse or success. Overall, probably much more effort in terms of people and material was put into the camouflage side of the equation, but seldom did it do more than delay discovery or temporarily divert some weapons during an attack.[2] In fairness, the camoufleurs were frequently given impossible tasks. Perhaps that is why their results sometimes displayed the naiveté of an ostrich trying to secure its head while leaving plenty unhidden to point the way to the critical part.

The following pages should give the reader a good idea which side was the overall winner in the game.

What is Camouflage

You cannot read much about World War II without running into the subject of camouflage. More correctly in modern terms, the subject should be divided into: camouflage, concealment and deception (CC&D). These three passive means of protecting places or things were often collectively referred to as camouflage. All three were actively and extensively used throughout WW II in attempts to shield vulnerable and valuable assets. (Unless

---

1. German aerial film was 11.8 inches wide; US film 9 inches wide or narrower; British aerial film was 7 inches wide or narrower. The huge German aerial exposures could record more of the earth at any given altitude and lens length than comparable Allied systems.

2. For example: the Germans made expensive, fantastically elaborate decoys that did not often fool anyone, but their paint work and direct installation camouflage was usually quite good. The Japanese used dazzle and toning paintwork that seldom blended with the surroundings but their decoys were often effective as confusion factors for aircrews. Also, towards the end of the war, roughly one out of every four planes on a Japanese airfield was probably a dummy. Additionally, both of these Axis nations made extensive and expert use of nets for camouflage. Finally, the Germans did not make extensive use of underground installations except where a cave might be available for use, but the Japanese were compulsive diggers, putting everything from factories and oil storage facilities to defence positions underground.

otherwise specified, this book uses WW II terminology in which camouflage includes all or any of the three aspects of CC&D.)

Everyone knows the basics of camouflage. We have all had the experience during a child's game of hiding ourselves, or some object. Hunters in the woods use camouflage. Women hide wrinkles and/or 'augment' their figures. All of that is camouflage – hiding something or making it look like something else. The principles are ancient and obvious. When played by nations, as in World War II, the game became much more sophisticated and more deadly. To lose the camouflage contest in war was to suffer the loss of some portion of one's capability to fight. Still, the basic rules of the child's game applied. You tried to convince your opponent that nothing of value was in a given place or that you were not going to do something you intended to do. Sometimes this was augmented by offering the opponent the suggestion that a target he expected was in some other location, or that you were about to take action different from your actual intentions.[3]

More specifically, camouflage in war became the disguising of places or things so they would not be detected, identified, or not fully understood by enemy intelligence, and to make them harder for attackers to hit.

The idea behind *Camouflage* was to paint or augment recognisable shapes to distort their recognition characteristics, or to make them blend into a background, thus rendering the subject 'invisible'. Proper blending could make the camouflaged asset 'disappear' to a casual or hurried observer, thus providing a level of passive protection, or, in the case of weapons systems, allow your ship, tank or plane to get closer to an enemy and initiate combat on your terms.

Concealment involved hiding an asset so it could not be seen, at least not seen directly. This could be done by putting the vehicle or factory inside a tunnel, under a complete blanket of netting, or under a camouflage construction that appeared to be something else. Of course the 'something else' had to be both innocent, such as a town or forest, and something that might reasonably occur at that location.

Deception included the positioning or simulation of things or activities to mislead an enemy as to their true location or function, or to mask some imminent course of action.[4] Deception was the most difficult of the three to pull off and was potentially the most profitable. The use of fake targets, simulating real ones nearby, might make an enemy spend ordnance in empty fields or mass forces to repel an attack in the wrong place. If they would only be viewed from a distance or fleetingly, decoys or dummies could be crude and made of simple materials. In other cases where the stakes were highest, such as prior to the 6 June 1944 Normandy landings, dummies used to simulate an invasion army in East Anglia were elaborate constructions of inflatable rubber, wood and metal that were surprisingly accurate copies of the real thing.

This trio of passive defences, widely used by all the warring nations in World War II, occurred most commonly in the nations on the defensive or having assets within reach of strategic weapons. Forces on the offensive had the initiative and had only to camouflage front-line assets that were in immediate jeopardy.[5]

Why Camouflage?

Military camouflage is based upon the old principle that 'you can't hit what you can't see'. A corollary might be 'you can't understand what you can't see'. In the giant, deadly game of hide-and-seek that was World War II, failure to hide or mask effectively resulted in detection and identification. To be detected, in turn, often resulted in either subsequent attack and destruction of critical assets or of a premature divulging of intentions. Early exposure of military intentions could also result in destruction of forces because it eliminated surprise and allowed the enemy to prepare a defence. Destruction of troops, equipment and supplies being massed for an attack, or loss of a capability being husbanded in a rear area for some later venture, were typical results of camouflage failure.

Was World War II Different in Use of Camouflage?

You bet WW II was different. Never before or since have warring nations used passive defences so extensively to protect combat and industrial value from enemy weapons.

Prior to about 1916, camouflage only had to be oriented to preclude horizontal observation. The most common means of camouflage in earlier times was simply to go behind a hill or tree-line, to dig trenches, light smoking fires or erect a tall screen to mask an enemy's view of actions taking place on or behind your side of the line of contact. Not only could camouflage be limited to the 180 degrees facing the enemy, it could be open on top. Balloon observers were used in the American Civil War and the Franco-Prussian War, but these were so few and far between that they had little affect on camouflage or combat except in highly localised situations.

The balloons were stationary, tethered behind their own lines. They could neither rise high enough, nor change position readily enough, to see much of what was going on beyond the front. Nor could they enter

---

3. Target is used in the intelligence sense: a subject for information collection. It may never be attacked.

4. Deceptions addressed in this book were physical, dealing with actual military assets or intentions. Other deceptions were bogus levels of communications traffic, fake radio messages, planted information 'leaks', and documents that were allowed to 'fall into enemy hands'.

5. In a protracted air war both sides could be on the offensive, bombing the heart of each other's territory, and on the defensive, defending and passively protecting their own assets from bombing.

enemy territory to view what was going on far to the rear.

Military use of the aeroplane changed everything. Even though the earliest warplanes could rise much higher and had the capability to range far, they were not used that way. Aircraft from both sides in WW I remained near the front, acting as artillery spotters and looking for signs of any build-up just behind the trenches. One reason for this was that the early planes could not carry enough of a bomb load to do more than annoy an enemy. Since aerial bombardment was so limited, artillery was the major weapon of choice. This, in turn, meant that there was little call for observers in planes to go beyond the range of one's heaviest guns (roughly 17–20 miles) to the rear.

Another reason for holding observation aircraft near the front was that while a single-seat aircraft had a good chance for survival in enemy air space, the pilot could not fly his plane, watch out for enemy planes, and still observe the ground in detail. On the other hand, crews of two-seaters could fly, watch and look, but their planes were so sluggish that they were easy prey for enemy pursuit aircraft.

Even at best the aerial observer system was only good for finding a few specific objectives. The observer could not remember enough, nor could he be expert enough, to be effective in searching a broad area of enemy territory for intelligence input of a general nature. Nor could a pilot or aerial observer reliably pass on to experts enough information, in enough detail or accuracy, to permit them to perform analysis on what was seen. The wide variety of highly specialised functions to be observed in an enemy country required a corresponding specialisation of analysis. This level of expert specialisation was far beyond the ability of a single observer. In addition, the large areas to be covered, and the subtle nature of early indicators of a build-up, needed detailed study over time and no aircrew dared spend this kind of time over a target.

Aerial photography provided the capability to go back and carefully study a place or thing, or compare what was seen today with earlier imagery. This study over time was invaluable to detailed analysis and understanding, particularly of complex subjects. To provide a host of rear-echelon experts the chance to look at specific parts of enemy territory, initially, the aerial observer was given a hand-held camera, but two-seat aircraft with cameras proved to be extremely vulnerable to enemy fighters and losses were high.

The answer came with the installation of automatic cameras in survivable, faster, more manoeuvrable, aircraft. Once images on glass plates brought back from behind enemy lines were printed, teams of specialists could spend whatever time was necessary to carefully examine the photos. Of course heavy glass plates severely limited the number of exposures that could be taken, but from this point on nothing a reconnaissance aircraft could over-fly was safe from observation. Nearly simultaneous implementation of

this type of photographic reconnaissance by both sides during WW I had an immediate impact on camouflage. After the use of aerial cameras became general, camouflage had to defend against viewing from overhead as well as horizontal observation.

The observation potential from roving aircraft meant that camouflage had to cover 360 degrees of viewing angle since the plane might approach from any direction and at any altitude (photo 1-2). This example, from a Soviet army manual on camouflage, shows that concessions had to be made to avoid aerial detection.[6] Keeping the gun barrel entirely inside the fake haystack seriously restricted space for the gun crew. So did keeping the camouflage net low over a gun, but as the drawing shows, the lower the net the better it hid the gun.

With ever-increasing speed and range, the aeroplane became more of a threat through the 1920s and 30s, and camouflage from vertical observation became correspondingly more important. As the

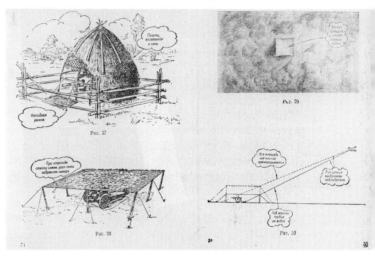

1-2 *Page from a Soviet Army manual on camouflage showing the reason to keep nets low and how to make a fake haystack as cover for an anti-tank gun.*

aeroplane acquired sufficient range to penetrate deep into enemy territory, the need for camouflage became more widespread, and new categories of installation needed to be protected. Aerial reconnaissance became strategic.

By World War II, aeroplanes were available with sufficient range, speed and altitude capability to penetrate well to the rear of any battle line, indeed, even into the heartland of most of the warring nations (UK, Germany, Soviet Union). The damage that could now be done from the air was so extensive that everyone wanted to hide from planes. It was also obvious that if a tactical or strategic target could be found from the air it could be destroyed from the air. The practice of camouflage flourished. For example,

6. The Soviet Army manual on camouflage was published in Moscow in 1942, captured by the Germans during their invasion of Russia, and acquired by American forces as part of the large collection of German intelligence materials found at the end of the war. The Soviet photo interpretation manual was published in Moscow in 1940, and found its way into US archives in the same manner.

1-3 Glass eyes for Allied Intelligence, Mount Farm, England, 1 July 1943. A pair of 24in-lensed K-17 cameras being loaded in the nose of an American F-5 photoreconnaissance aircraft (reconnaissance version of the P-38). These cameras each held enough film for 250 9x9in. exposures.

by 1944 the US Army had nearly 500 Engineer Camouflage Battalions and had gone from none in 1943 to 600 Aviation Camouflage Battalions.

Cameras were good enough, and photo interpretation techniques developed enough, to find the nuances of information that made for good intelligence analysis. Film emulsions coated on flexible material allowed rolls of from 200 to 500 exposures and this meant that much larger areas could be covered. The cameras could now mount lenses up to a yard long which enabled detailed views from high altitude.

These advances made WW II different from any previous war because, by 1940, aerial photo-reconnaissance made virtually anything in any part of a country that could be overflown identifiable and therefore vulnerable.

During WW II, each belligerent sought on unprecedented scales to mask production capacity, technical developments, build-up of forces, and movements of combat power, from enemy intelligence. Camouflage and deception were major contributors to these goals.

Towards the end of World War II, technology began to supersede visual air attack and straight visual photo interpretation. Radar and other electronics made navigation and target acquisition problems of science rather than eyeballs. Infra-red, false-colour, and colour film made finding cut branches, nets, and

other camouflage a matter of simple recognition rather than arcane skills.[7] These trends continued through the post-war years as new decades brought new heights in technology.

Subsequent developments brought increased emphasis on electronic sensors and exotic film to penetrate the secrets of enemy places and equipment, thus rendering strategic and large-area camouflage all but useless. This makes the years from 1939 to early 1945 the 'Glory Days' of camouflage against aerial observation, and of the visual photo interpreter. Never before was camouflage so needed. Never afterwards did camouflage have such a chance of success against technology. During those WW II years the odds in the game were almost even. Expertise, determination and attention to detail determined whether camouflage or intelligence would win in any encounter.

Photo Intelligence

The main adversary of any camouflage or deception programme was enemy intelligence. The most versatile and effective tool of the intelligence opponents of camouflage was the partnership of high-performance aircraft, aerial cameras and photo interpretation (photos 1-3 and 1-4). The glass eye of the aerial camera was pitted against enemy artists, engineers, craftsmen, and soldiers on the ground. By 1940 aerial photo interpretation had grown from a tool of map-makers and tactical operations specialists to a full-fledged discipline in its own right. Experts in weapons systems, transportation, industry, engineering and military operations began to study otherwise denied enemy territory in unprecedented detail from overhead. Experience quickly demonstrated that these photo interpreters

1-4 The real enemy of camouflage: a photo interpreter. This US Army officer is shown examining his photo prints using a stereoscope which also provided 3X magnification.

---

7. Special films were specifically intended to find camouflage. Colour film could record changes in tone that black-and-white film might not make apparent. Infra-red (IR) film reacted differently to live and dead vegetation. Cut branches so commonly used as a fast, easy tactical camouflage showed up in sharp contrast on IR film.

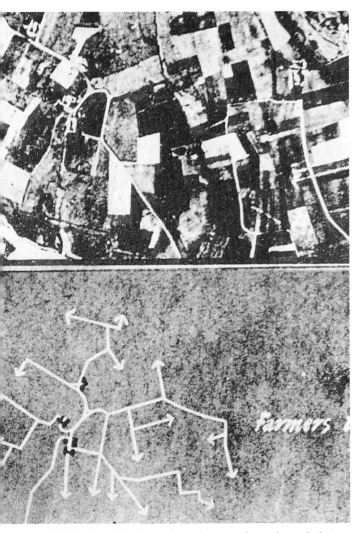

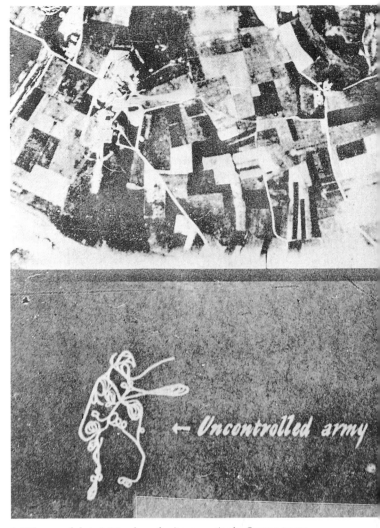

1-5 Man's activity almost always leaves marks on the earth that are interpretable from the air. In the spring of 1940, French farmers left paths as they moved around field boundaries to avoid trampling crops (From a 1941 British manual on photo interpretation).

1-6 The area of photo 1-5 ten days after its occupation by German troops in June 1940. Military movements created paths that disregarded field boundaries.

could extract amazing levels of information from aerial photography.

For the trained expert, everything man does on the face of the earth leaves a trace. These marks could be paths that school children made through fields, unique buildings characteristic of a certain industry, lines of transportation, turned earth from a buried cable or farm boundaries (photo 1-5). The scars on the ground might be revetments for guns, the tonal change of a fire-gutted structure or tracks left on grass by the movement of military vehicles (photo 1-6). Often the size of the building or revetment, or width of a track would permit identification of a function, gun type and calibre, or vehicle type.

Sometimes the clue used by the photo interpreter was not the object or a mark on the ground. The shadow of the object often gave it away (photo 1-7). In this example, 20 ineptly parked trucks could be spotted without difficulty. This can also be viewed as a breach of camouflage discipline since it was human error that led to the vehicles being more vulnerable. The same trucks were harder to locate when they were parked so their shadows merged into the

surrounding landforms (photo 1-8). An aerial observer or PI not expecting vehicles in this area might overlook the better placed trucks.

One of the most difficult problems faced by a photo interpreter is the understanding that marks or shadows on the earth might either be mundane or could be of vital military significance. The aerial camera captured everything – the normal and the important – and it was the PI who had to sort it all out. In many cases these traces of man's interaction with the earth were characteristic to the point of being keys to identifying the related activity. Characteristic marks, shapes or arrangements of buildings or alignments of objects were known as 'signatures' (photo 1-9).

A trained photo interpreter knew how to spot the most important signatures. Their presence told him what was going on even when he could not see the activity in detail. The more experienced the PI, the more signatures he could cope with. Signatures were the keys for a photo interpreter to identify various types of military and industrial targets with a high degree of credibility. Signature clues labelled

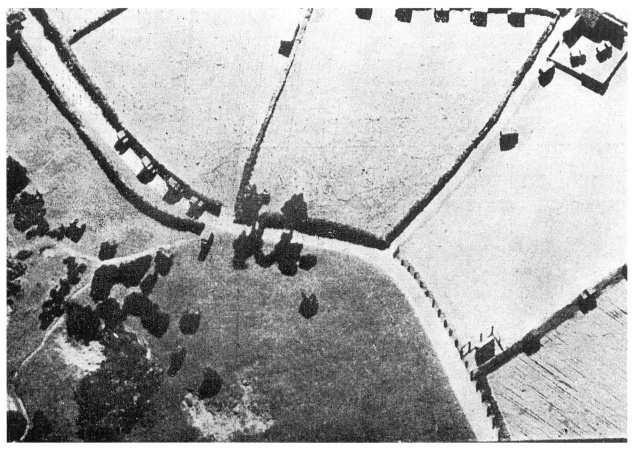

1-7 Page from a 1942 British manual on camouflage. This demonstration showed 20 trucks parked where they were easy to see from the air.

1-8 Part two of the British camouflage demonstration in 1942. The same 20 trucks parked on the same ground as in photo 1-7, but this time with attention to their shadows and visibility. (If you can't find all of the trucks, see Appendix II.)

one complex as a steel mill, another an oil refinery, and still another as an ammunition factory – and those are only a few of the more obvious examples.

Military activity had signatures too, but here the PI had to know a great deal about enemy equipment and its operational employment. The number, size, shape and arrangement of revetments could permit a PI to discriminate between a medium anti-aircraft battery and one of heavy howitzers. The distance across a battery could even allow identification of gun calibre, and therefore specific type – this allowed operations personnel to plan more effectively, taking into consideration the full capability of the enemy battery.

The identification game really got tricky when the proper signatures were presented on purpose but were, in reality, bogus – and this is where camouflage and deception came in. Dummies were great when they worked. When they did not, they just tipped the enemy off that there was a reason to deceive and the enemy started looking harder for that reason. Bogus objects or facilities were also extensively used during the air war to draw enemy ordnance or attention away from real assets.

'The Big Green Ball' is huge, and installations or activities one might like to know about can occur anywhere. Keeping watch on places and things you already know about was one thing; finding previously unknown targets was another matter entirely. Finding an unknown, possibly entirely new, activity or weapons system was hard enough when it was expected (tipped off by electronic intelligence or spies) and a general location provided. Identifying such sites where they were not expected was a cross between raw luck and some of the most drudging work an intelligence analyst could perform.

The primary need was good quality, comprehensive aerial photography of any key area to be studied. Of course, regular aerial photo coverage was needed of front lines or known industrial and military complexes. But this type of coverage concentrated analysis on areas or activities that were already known, or suspected from other sources such as signals intelligence or agent reports. A more sophisticated use of the aerial camera involved 'trolling' through an enemy held area. In this method of reconnaissance, the mission photographed strips of previously, or infrequently, covered territory

where new activities might have been expected. Every inch of the imagery would then be carefully screened under magnification in a search for anything suspicious. High flying reconnaissance aircraft could carry cameras that scooped up coverage far to either side of the flight track through many miles of forward travel.[8] Trolling was used to expand the area an intelligence organisation understood. It was also how new installations, material being amassed for an attack, or new weapon systems were often located. Of course, these were the very objectives each side tried hardest to keep from disclosure to their enemy.

One of the most effective photo-intelligence techniques for watching known targets, finding new ones, and penetrating camouflage was the use of comparative photo coverage (the other being use of stereoscopic viewing). This meant that an area would be covered periodically over time. Detailed comparison of the photos would allow a photo interpreter to pinpoint changes. The changes, in turn, could be indicators of trends or clues to enemy intentions. An increase in the supplies stored in a dump could mean an offensive. A change in raw materials at a factory probably meant a corresponding change in production. An addition changing the shape of a small forest probably indicated a hidden installation built since the last photo coverage.

A detailed understanding of what was happening on the enemy side of the line was made more difficult when signatures were muddled, covered or obscured by disguise. That was one of the major missions of camouflage, concealment and deception.

Stopping the Bomber

In the late 1930s conventional wisdom held that 'the bomber can always get through'.[9] Unlike intelligence analysts, who generally viewed a target from directly overhead with no time constraints on the viewing [10], the bomber's view was quite different – fleeting and more oblique.

On the threshold of war, governments feared that all of their military and industrial resources would lie naked beneath streams of raiding bombers. Since there was little confidence in active defences, passive defences became more important. Grasping at anything to protect assets in the face of what seemed

8. The area covered depended upon the number of cameras involved, the lens length used, aircraft altitude, and the length of film carried in each camera magazine. Using 250 feet of film in each of three K-17 cameras with 6-inch lenses, a US F-5 reconnaissance plane flying at 23,000 feet could collect 6,000 square miles of usable coverage in a single mission. Of course, images near the edges of each photo were smaller and less distinct than those more nearly below the aircraft – and thus less lucrative from the intelligence standpoint.

9. In actual practice this did not prove to be the case unless the side doing the bombing also had control of the air. Prophets of strategic bombing, such as Brig. Gen. William 'Billy' Mitchell and Italy's Gen. Giulio Douhet, worked to convince the world that nothing could stop a modern bomber force ('The bomber will always get through'). In the early 30s they were right when some light and medium bombers had the speed of pursuit ships. This speed advantage made air interception virtually impossible without advanced warning to let pursuit planes climb into attack position ahead of the

bombers – and radar was not yet available. By 1939 pursuit-plane technology had caught up. Not only did the single-seater once again have enough speed advantage to intercept, but radar was available to guarantee a meeting. By 1941 the bomber could only get through at night unless high losses could be accepted. Eventually, radar, particularly airborne intercept radar, began to close down the night raiding bombers as well. Towards the end of WW II, bombers could 'get through' with impunity only if they could fly higher than the defending fighters (like B-29s over Japan) or were escorted by their own fighter planes (like B-17s and B-24s over Germany).

10. The Allies commonly did PI work on photographic prints. It took longer to get prints out of the Lab, but they allowed stereoscopic viewing. German PIs used prints and stereo viewing only in later phases of the photo-intelligence cycle, such as preparing in-depth studies of a given function. See my book *World War II Photo Intelligence*.

STORES DUMP

In the AMERSFOORT (Holland) stores dump the close packing of the stacks should be noted as distinct from the typical lay-out of ammunition dumps. The main buildings have been extensively camouflaged.

A typical example of the more permanent type of ammunition dump and filling factory is seen at CHATEAUDUN, France. Note the dispersal of stacks and the extensive light railway system.

801.142

1-9 Page from a British study on camouflage showing the look of a typical supply and ammunition dump. Characteristics like these are called 'signatures' by photo interpreters and, if supported by enough detail, serve to identify an installation – or separate the real from the dummy.

to be certain destruction, camouflage was one of the most natural and most readily implemented passive defences.[11]

In fact, camouflage did work well against crews bombing visually, if it was done correctly. Approaching at nearly 200 mph and flying at 15,000 (4,600 m) to 25,000 feet (7,600 m), the pilot and bomb-aimer had a mutual timing problem. To bomb at that speed and altitude, the release point was roughly two to three miles out in front of the target. Target acquisition had to occur within 30 seconds prior to release, or four to five miles from the target.

Check points such as rivers, coastline, or other prominent physical or cultural features could be used to narrow down the search for the target. However,

made to camouflage landmarks. If camouflage could confuse the aircrew for a mere 10 to 20 seconds, bomb aiming would not be as accurate and the target might survive.

How to Camouflage

One early World War II book on camouflage recalled an old US Army engineer NCO describing camouflage as, 'Makin' 'em think you are where you ain't and not lett'n 'em know where you are'.

Most camouflage was just good common sense, albeit sense based upon the knowledge and experience of the camoufleur. Another page from the Soviet manual on camouflage illustrates how really effective camouflage could be achieved with very

1-10 The Soviet camouflage manual showed how to hide a gun using simple techniques and available cover.

to be bombed, the location of the target had to be positively identified.[12] Camouflage was extensively and intensively used to make it difficult for aircrews to pick a target out of its background. Since locational relationships with nearby landmarks could give away a target location, attempts were sometimes

little effort (photo 1-10). The three anti-tank gun positions, in different situations, had one thing in common: simplicity of implementation. A little paint to simulate the shadows of boards on the gun shield added considerably to the effect in a destroyed building. A few logs laid about in front of the haystacks made the gun barrel less obvious. An earth-coloured tarpaulin over a small gully provided cover from observation. The manual even showed how to fold the tarp back on one side to permit rain water to drain rather than collapsing the camouflage – a problem that defeated some of the most elaborate and extensive camouflage jobs.

11. The other most commonly employed passive defence for a known large target was a version of concealment: a smoke screen.

12. This was different from actually seeing the target – which was, of course the best aiming situation. If a target could be accurately located by its relationships to other things around it, that target might be bombed even though it was completely covered with camouflage or otherwise obscured. This is the principle used in 'radar offset' bombing which became a stand-by for the US Strategic Air Command during the Cold War.

Можно уменьшить заметность материальной части с воздуха, расположив ее около забора, при условии установки объектов не в тени забора, а, наоборот, с солнечной стороны, чтобы тень от объектов сливалась с тенью от забора

(рис. 58). Нельзя располагать маскируемые объекты в тени предметов, которые ниже их, так как тень от них тогда не будет скрыта. При расположении объектов около канавы их также следует ставить с солнечной стороны, с таким расчетом, чтобы тень от объектов падала на канаву.

Рис. 56. Установка объектов в тени зданий.

Рис. 58. Установка объектов около заборов:
а — правильно; б — неправильно.

При движении автотранспорта по дороге (при одностороннем движении) нужно двигаться с таким расчетом, чтобы тень падала не на дорогу, а на канаву или на траву.

ПРИМЕНЕНИЕ МАСКИРОВОЧНОГО МАТЕРИАЛА

Применение к местности, являясь основой маскировки всех военных объектов, не дает достаточного эффекта без дополнительных мероприятий, к которым в первую очередь относится применение срезанной растительности — того естественного материала, который всегда находится под руками.

Маскировочный материал (срезанная растительность) при правильном применении и уходе за ним с трудом будет поддаваться дешифровке.

Необходимо помнить, что срезанные хвойные ветви много темнее лиственных; при воздушном наблюдении разница в цвете хвойных и лиственных пород ясно различима. При расположении объектов в лиственном лесу не сле-

Рис. 57. Установка объекта под маскировочным навесом.

1-11 Page from a Soviet army pamphlet on aerial photo interpretation showing how a plane could be hidden next to a house and the use of natural shadows from a house and a fence to hide a plane and a truck.

The abiding rule of camouflage has always been: 'blend in'. If a target stood out against its background it was sure to be caught. This meant blending had to address every aspect of the clues a photo interpreter or ground observer would use to find a target. Certainly the object itself had to be hidden, but to be really effective, so did its shadow, and any route, track or line that led to it (photo 1-11). The example, from a Soviet manual on photo interpretation, showed how a plane or truck might be hidden in the shadow of a house and fence. Another technique, illustrated in the manual, was the use of netting to hide a tell-tale shadow.

At the most rudimentary level, camouflage was a rifleman using some cut twigs in his helmet to make himself less conspicuous or less of a target to an enemy rifleman. Of course, at the tactical level, camouflage is more directed against horizontal viewing than concern for a camera overhead. This time-honoured, tactical and very traditional use of camouflage was easily extended from the individual up to larger assets such as tanks, ships or aircraft. All these potential targets were mobile and their mobility added strength to any camouflage they might get. This was particularly true when the mobile asset took up a new position at a site where it had not been before. A camouflaged object that was unsuspected

had a far better chance of escaping detection.

Tactical camouflage could be very pragmatic, using simple material at hand (photo 1-12). It might just involve covering a gun position, then making sure that the blast from the muzzle did not beat down vegetation to give the position away. Another precaution was camouflage discipline. That is, insuring that troops did nothing that would degrade the camouflage.

An example of camouflage discipline would involve the contrast of a good and poor defence position on the same ground (photo 1-13). In the first case the trenches show clearly from their strong shadows and newly-turned spoil. The trench lines were situated with no thought of the surrounding landforms or cultural features. Finally, troops returning from the road had made prominent paths showing where they were positioned.

In the second case, the trenches had been situated to conform to the existing land and had netting covering trenches and freshly-turned earth (photo 1-14). As a final touch, in ideal (if unrealistic) camouflage discipline, troops going to the gun from a road or latrine would be ordered to walk right past the position to some other road or path, then reach the trenches by doubling back on their route. They would be intentionally making an obvious path that

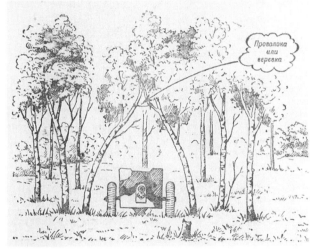

1-12 Soviet army guidance on camouflaging an anti-tank gun position in tree cover.

1-13 British model of a defence position poorly related to its background. Trenches, freshly turned earth, and paths are obvious.

1-14 The defence position of photo 1-13 situated to fit into the lines of the background pattern. Trenches were covered and paths passed through, rather than stopped at, the troop positions.

bypassed their positions. In this way no clear path was worn to give away the real position.

It was hard enough to maintain tactical camouflage discipline, but it was considerably more difficult to hide a factory, port, city or airfield. This was particularly true if the installation was well known to an enemy from pre-war days. Of course, the problem was doubled in difficulty if the installation had to remain in operation under its camouflage. Some really amazing examples of the art of camouflage rose from this challenge. Using fishnet, burlap, coloured canvass, wood and other simple materials, whole factories and harbours were transformed into farm fields, city streets or tree studded hills.

Sometimes the best that could be done for a fixed installation was to tone down the target so it was less conspicuous. Toning might make a target harder to see and thus cut a bomber's aiming time, especially in night air raids. Sometimes the camouflage task was recognised as impossible and, to make the best of a bad situation, a decoy installation was offered to enemy bombers. The decoy would usually be positioned so the enemy would come upon it before they would see the real target. The idea was that the

1-15 Early WW II camouflage was often done with more art and enthusiasm than effectiveness. These British hangars were carefully painted to look like houses, but the obvious concrete parking ramps gave the hangars away.

decoy might split an attack, drawing some ordnance away from the real target. Sometimes it worked. The chances of a decoy succeeding were much better when the enemy was bombing at night.

A rash of books and pamphlets published in the early months of World War II gave advice on how to camouflage towns and factories. Most of this information was more idealistic than helpful. For example, one of the most advocated techniques was to plant trees and bushes around and on top of factories. This did a nice job of hiding a building – if the roof could stand the weight – but the camoufleurs commonly ignored approaching roads, railways and walks.

Another common technique was to paint the buildings in disruptive patterns. As WW II began, artists, theatre people and architects offered their services, wanting to help out. They brought unique skills to the camouflage problem, but few of them had ever seen the earth from a plane. Most of their work was imaginative and expertly executed, but of little use (photo 1-15). Buildings all over the world were splashed with irregular bands of colour that were supposed to make them invisible to aircrew.

Where construction was used to augment paint, the dilettante experts usually made marvellously complicated and detailed covering camouflage. In 1939–40 it was not uncommon to have camouflage so elaborate and blanketing that it hindered the operation of what was being hidden. Seldom were any provisions made to tie the localised camouflage into the ground or eliminate the shadows cast by the buildings, though neither of these were particularly hard to do (photos 1-16 and 1-17). The neophyte

1-16 The lines of a roof nicely broken up by simple construction work – but the shadow was unaffected and the paint job did not blend the building into the ground. Mitchell Field, New York, 23 February 1943.

camoufleurs simply did not realise that incomplete blending with a total environment could be worse than no camouflage at all.

Shadows often marked the location of a gun position or building more clearly than direct observation of the structure (photo 1-18). If the camouflage subject was underground or low, the best technique to eliminate shadows was a low covering

20

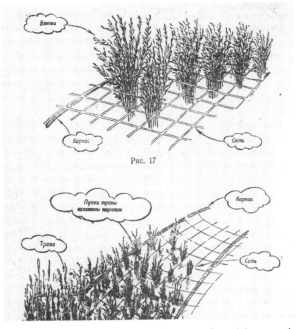

1-17 *Page from the Soviet army manual on camouflage giving examples of using freshly cut natural material to garnish netting and how to blend a net into the ground.*

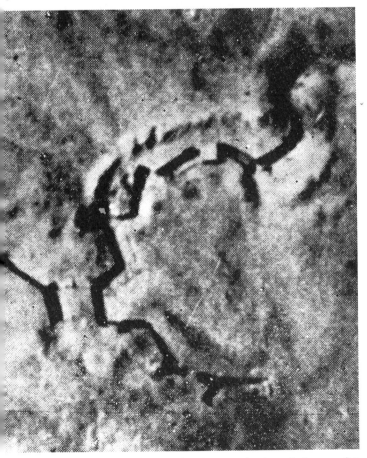

1-18 *Desert positions were often given away by strong shadows on a flat, plain background.*

on the trench or structure (photo 1-19). When the objective had to have work space around it, or was too tall to simply cover, the best solution was to install an umbrella of netting to disrupt an aerial view of the subject and its shadow (photo 1-20). This tanker would have been better camouflaged if the netting had sloped all the way to the ground. Apparently camouflage experts on the ground did not realise that by using stereo viewing techniques a PI could literally see right through most netting.

Another consideration in painted camouflage was that pigments normally maintained tone and colour value for three to four months. If painted camouflage was not regularly renewed it became counter-productive, serving to highlight the building rather than hide it. It was equally inadvisable to paint some roofs in a building complex and not others. Paint camouflage in a sea of roofs only served to identify the buildings with military significance (photo 1-21).

Painting patterns that extended to the surrounding ground were more effective than simple painting, but on natural surfaces the pigments lasted for a mere two to three weeks. Again, if not renewed this camouflage became detrimental. Later in the war, the US Army conducted tests indicating that toning a camouflage subject with a plain dull colour was just as effective as pattern painting.

Some of the early war camouflage advice was pretty good. People were instructed to avoid straight lines or circles as these shapes are not found in nature. They were also told to break up the unnatural lines of nearby roads and buildings that called attention to the subject being camouflaged. The most important lesson was to avoid doing good camouflage work on just part of an installation. One of the most common errors was to divide a camouflage job into segments completed by different people. This could lead to excellent camouflage in one part of an installation and poor work in another (photo 1-22). Poor work always negated the good. To be effective, camouflage had to be both good and thorough in its cover of a target (photo 1-23).

Another give-away occurred when camouflage just did not look right in its overall context. An example was a Japanese cruiser found by American PIs in 1945 (photo 1-24). The ragged Japanese coastline suddenly became an outline of smooth convex scallops. Normal tonal transitions from shallow to deep water suddenly changed to a direct jump from shore to a deep water tone. Things like that catch a PI's eyes, and once attention was called to the area the straight line where the netting was tented along the centre of the hull was easy to see (photo 1-25). The cruiser's class could be roughly judged by measuring the length of the camouflage hidden shape.[13]

Back to Moscow

Another German photo mission over Moscow, this one on 5 October 1941, illustrates many of the points made above. First there is the value of comparison between this coverage and the 22 July photo that opened this chapter. Any improvements or

---

13. The ship was identified as a Kuma or Natori-class light cruiser. These classes were just a few feet different in length and beam. *Kitakami* was the only ship left in either class by July 1945.

intervening damage would be easy to pick out. A plot of the mission showed that the Luftwaffe reconnaissance plane had little trouble lining up on the heart of the city (photo 1-26). The Kremlin and

Red Square might be camouflaged but the river was not and it could be used to locate them. Nor were the actual targets – Moscow's Central Airfield on frame 82 and the inland port facilities on frame 88 – camouflaged in any way.

A closer look at Red Square shows that the painted buildings were fading (photo 1-27).[14] Not only was this camouflage less effective than it had been in July, but the painted shadows no longer came close to the reality of longer winter shadows. Really good painted camouflage had to be redone to match seasonal changes.

A photo taken in Red Square on 7 November 1941, during the annual parade honouring the October Revolution, shows how simple the painted buildings really were (photo 1-28).[15] This also illustrates how distance eliminates the need for detail. The rough lines of the painted shadows appeared as sharp, straight lines to the aircrew and camera overhead.

Moving to an even greater enlargement, magnification a German PI could barely attain using

14. The photo was taken at 0834 hours, Moscow time. A light morning frost on the paintwork did not help what was left to look more effective.

15. In spite of a rapidly advancing German Army, Stalin decided to hold the parade in 1941 as a demonstration that 'everything was normal'.

1-19 (Left) Page from a 1941 British manual on camouflage in the desert with examples of low nets used to kill shadows.

1-20 Camouflage netting set high to cover and kill shadows at a refuelling point during manoeuvres in the US, 1943. (National Archives)

1-21 Camouflage could be counterproductive if it served to tell the enemy where military objectives were hidden amid civilian structures. American B-25s of the 345th Bomber Group had no trouble locating the key Japanese buildings at Rabaul on 2 November 1943.

1-22 A four-gun US coastal defence battery, Taboga Island, Panama, 6 November 1943. Only one of the guns was under good camouflage – and the guns in the open called attention to the spot and thus gave away the whole battery.

1-24 (Below, bottom) On 5 July 1945, US photo interpreters of XXI Bomber Command found a well-covered Japanese light cruiser near Kure, Japan, because the lines they saw 'did not belong'.

1-25 (Below ,top) Enlargement of photo 1-24 showing the flaws in this camouflage job. The lines of the camouflage were too even and the tones too sharp when compared to the normal irregular outlines and gradual shading from beach to deep water.

1-23 US Coastal Artillery troops running to man their well-camouflaged guns, Chachachacare, British West Indies, June 1942. (DAVA-USArmy)

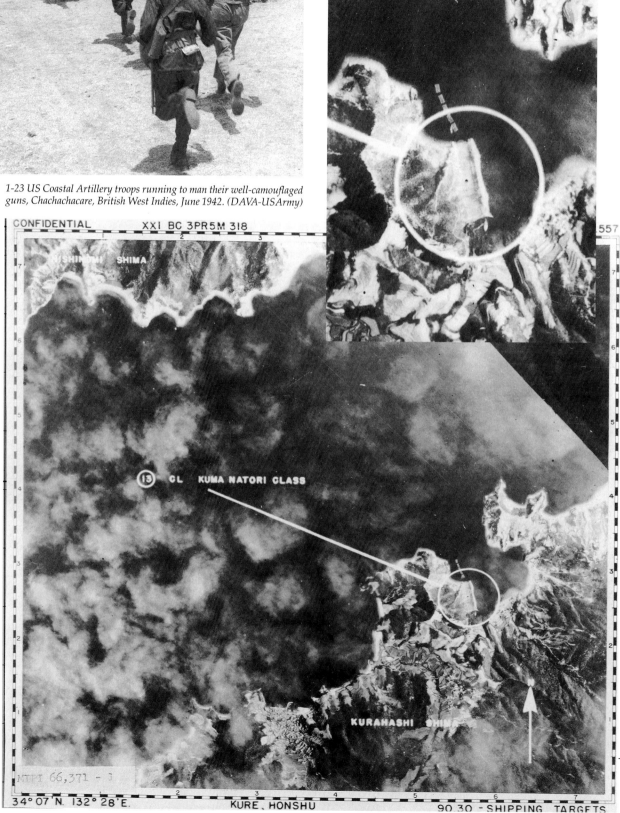

CONFIDENTIAL   XXI BC 3PR5M 318

CL   KUMA NATORI CLASS

KURAHASHI SHIMA

34° 07'N. 132° 28'E.   KURE, HONSHU   90.30 -SHIPPING TARGETS

24

his most powerful lens, shows more detail of the Kremlin camouflage (photo 1-29). Since July, some roofs had been painted with dark lines that were supposed to simulate streets in shadow, to make the Kremlin look like just another part of the surrounding city blocks.

Did the Kremlin camouflage work? No, but it was not a bad try in a nearly hopeless situation. There were simply too many factors working against the task of hiding such a well known landmark. Other efforts, in other places, tried just as hard to protect key targets. Other aircrew and intelligence organisations tried just as hard to find the targets. Some camouflage was successful, some was so inept it was humorous. The succeeding chapters will deal with the good, the bad and the unusual as throughout the world the deadly game was played for various categories of target.

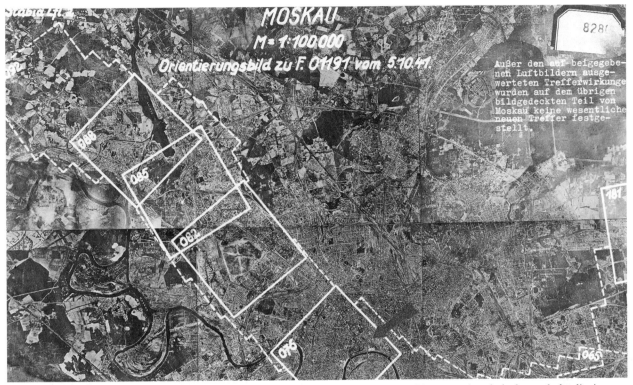

1-26 German orientation graphic showing the coverage of a 5 October 1941 photo mission over Moscow against the background of earlier imagery. The arrow shows the location of the camouflaged Kremlin and Red Square.

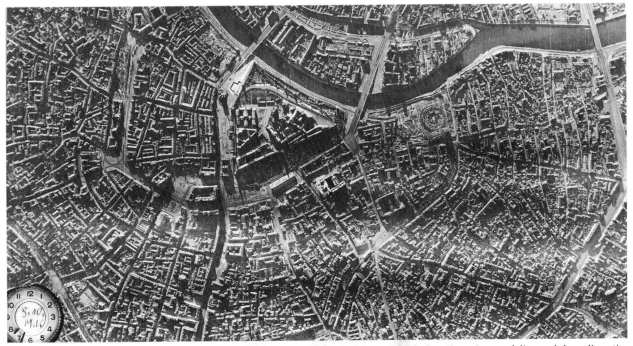

1-27 German coverage of Moscow, 5 October 1941. The painted camouflage on Red Square's bricks from the spring was fading, and shape-disrupting bands of dark paint had been added to Kremlin roofs.

1-28 Painted buildings in Red Square were nothing more than crudely done shadows and shading. (Photo probably from the October Revolution Parade, 7 November 1941).

1-29 Enlargement of photo 1-27. Painted shadows of fake buildings no longer came close to the angle or length of real shadows.

CHAPTER 2

DOWN TO EARTH

Camouflage of Land Warfare Assets

As the chapter title implies, camouflage of land warfare assets was a matter of realistic effort to blend with the ground on a very localised scale. This was not the camouflage of huge building complexes, long lines of communication or great ports. This level of camouflage involved the hiding of small groups of combatants and their equipment, usually in a tactical environment.

No one was more pragmatic about camouflage than the individual front-line soldier. If some rear-echelon engineer's fancy idea for camouflage weighed too much or got in the way of easy movement, or was a bother to maintain, then the front-line troops would ignore it. One popular method of getting rid of unwanted equipment was simply to 'lose' it.[1] If, on the other hand, the camouflage paraphernalia, technique or clothing increased his chances of staying alive, the soldier would go to great lengths to use it for himself and his equipment.

Hiding the Soldier

The soldier's basic camouflage protection was his drab uniform. Each of the warring nations painted their equipment and dressed their armies in dull shades of tan, grey, brown or green. Occasionally troops were provided with a uniform or overall made in a mottled or random multi-coloured camouflage pattern (photo 2-1). The German soldier in this 1941 example was a sniper in Russia. His pattern-camouflaged jacket and helmet cover were topped off with a fringe-like face mask that may have been of local fabrication. Individual soldiers were always augmenting their basic

2-1 German sniper in a mottled camouflage uniform and wearing a face mask to improve his cover. Soviet Union, 1942.

1. Gas masks were the classic example of a piece of World War II gear conveniently lost by troops all over the world. Soldiers who did not mislay them entirely tossed out their masks and used the case to carry things they felt they needed more.

2-2 Chinese troops under colour-stained rough hemp netting. This was poor camouflage because it was too dark to blend with the surrounding ground.

uniform with natural or artificial material to improve their chances of disappearing into the background.

One of the most common and simplest camouflage augmentations was a coloured net (photo 2-2). The example photo, taken in China in 1941, shows the nets well but also shows that these were too dark to be effective where they were being used. The lesson is that netting had to blend with the ground or it was worse than useless – it called attention rather than hid.

Better camouflage was demonstrated by the Japanese in China in 1938 (photo 2-3). Japanese assault troops garnished their packs with grass and small branches. As they crawled slowly forward this

2-3 Japanese assault troops camouflaged with freshly cut brush, China, 1938.

natural material would mask their bulk and help their mustard-coloured uniforms blend with the ground. Helmet nets were issued to all armies and covering a helmet with twigs, leaves and small branches was a universal camouflage technique. Larger branches were used to hide tanks, guns, and foxholes. Of course this camouflage is short term. When the uprooted vegetation wilts it must be replaced.

In what may be the ultimate in individual camouflage, Soviet partisans came up with a dark green overall and head covering liberally garnished with strands of cloth and hemp (photo 2-4). A man dressed in this suit would lie motionless, allowing German soldiers to pass by, then he was free to attack them from the rear. So well did this suit blend into a forest background that German intelligence felt it was necessary to annotate the photo with an outline of the standing figure. As with all camouflage, even the partisan suit did not perform well out of its intended environment (photo 2-5). A bush walking around in the open with a rifle was sure to attract attention.

Winter

Snow cover presented ground combat people with a special problem. One contemporary book on camouflage quoted an old US Army Engineer pointing out that without due care, troops 'stood out like a fly in a glass of milk'. The dark-toned drab uniforms that served to blend soldiers into their background most of the year could be a real detriment in winter.

2-4 German soldier posing in a sniper suit taken from a Russian partisan, Chertezh, Soviet Union, 1941.

2-5 A suit similar to photo 2-4. In a more open background this highly specialised camouflage was counterproductive.

To solve this problem, troops were dressed in white overalls, which also added another layer of clothing for warmth. The best of these winter uniforms had the additional advantage of being waterproof. Gear, like helmets, was often whitewashed or painted white (photo 2-6). Sometimes weapons and gear would be wrapped in white cloth to help hide them against a snow background (photo 2-7). Major pieces of equipment, like tanks and guns, were also whitened for camouflage. The whitewash or cheap paint had to be continually refreshed or the effect soon faded (photo 2-8).

Winter camouflage nets were issued to some units, but were never plentiful (photo 2-9). White camouflage nets were very effective. They were actually enhanced by snowfall where regular camouflage netting failed badly. When winter netting was not available, any white cloth would do and troops were not shy about obtaining what they needed (photo 2-10). The white sheet treatment was a good idea, but positioning of a vehicle was important too (photo 2-11).

In photo 2-9 the truck was in the middle of a snowbound field and only its shadow might give it away. In photo 2-11 the half-tracks were parked, by habit, along a field boundary line. This positioning was good during the rest of the year, but with snow covering the ground these vehicles stood out rather than blended. In winter camouflage, being out in the open was often better than being adjacent to existing cover.

Winter also complicated camouflage of tactical installations. White camouflage might be used to cover individual vehicles or gun positions, but tracks had to be considered more than ever (photo 2-12). In this example panels of white cloth did a credible job of hiding a four-gun US heavy artillery battery in

Italy, but tracks gave the positions away. The two guns sited at upper left were badly betrayed. The one at lower right had its camouflage weakened by the tracks of vehicles turning. Only the gun nearest the town on the right was emplaced with proper attention to camouflage discipline. At this gun position no undue tracks resulted because the local road system was used to move in the weapon and turn the prime mover and ammunition trucks.

For a unit without an ample supply of white camouflage material, the best winter cover was afforded by finding a sheltered place where snow cover was sparse. If such a site could be found, regular camouflage materials and techniques could be used effectively (photo 2-13). In this example, olive drab tents showed plainly against the snow, but the netting-covered command post was all but invisible. Of course, the tents would call suspicion to the area. If the enemy had any comparative photo cover, the changes would have been obvious and this site would have been found without much trouble.

Fixed Weapon Sites

Every army had garrisons, depots, training camps and all the other fixed installations necessary to the existence of a peacetime military force. These sites were generally too well known and seldom important enough to warrant camouflage once war began. When a few did get some camouflage treatment it was usually the bare minimum, such as a simple paint job (photo 2-14). A little dazzle-paint cover did not hide much when the security fence line

2-6 German soldiers with winter camouflage coveralls over their grey uniforms, Gzhatsk, Soviet Union, December 1942.

29

2-7 Soviet troops in winter coveralls. Even the anti-tank rifle was wrapped in white.

2-8 German Tiger tank whitewashed for winter, Taytsy, Soviet Union, February 1942.

2-10 A three-inch gun of the US 75th Infantry Division camouflaged with a 'liberated' lace table cloth, Belgium, 13 January 1945. (DAVA-USArmy)

2-11 Half-tracks of the US 10th Armoured Division near Bastogne, Belgium, under sheets borrowed from local civilians; 29 December 1944. (DAVA-USArmy)

2-9 US 2½ ton truck covered by a white camouflage net, Luxembourg, 8 January 1945. Light snow and frost add to the effect. (DAVA-USArmy)

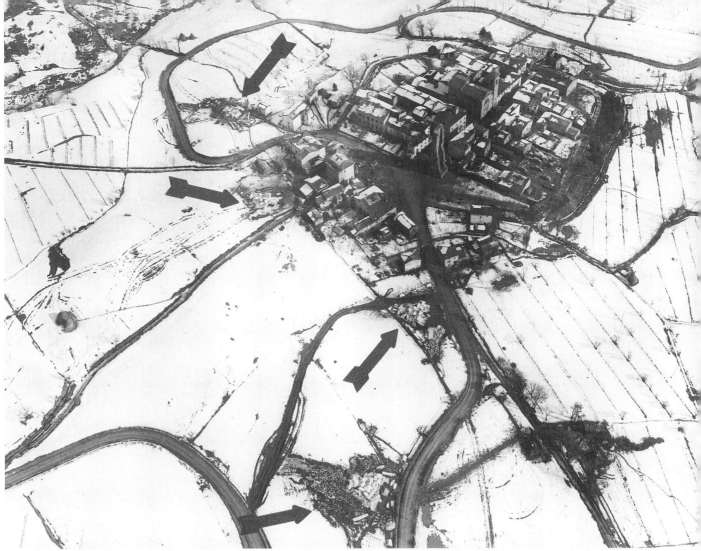

2-12 White panels over regular netting disguised a four-gun 155mm 'Long Tom' battery at Castel di Casio, Italy, 5 February 1945. Track activity spoiled the camouflage effectiveness, but the two positions nearest the town were well situated to hide in the local road pattern. (DAVA-USArmy)

2-13 Camouflaged command post of the XI Corps in Italy, 11 January 1945. The tents on the right might have called attention to the area but the real target was nicely blended into a mottled background. (DAVA-USArmy)

2-14 German barracks area on the Baltic coast under dazzle camouflage paint, 9 October 1943.

showed so well and interior walkways were not even toned down.

Fixed positions for major defence weapons were another matter. These were camouflaged as a rule, despite their locations being known from pre-war days. The simplest camouflage was to keep the position low and allow grass to grow up around the site (photo 2-15). Another technique was to mask a site from horizontal observation using a revetment that blended into the surroundings (photo 2-16). These sites for heavy coastal defence guns were generally designed in the 1920s, or earlier. Their construction showed they were built before aerial observation and attack were fully appreciated. These defensive works were designed against a horizontal threat from warships. Camouflage against an aerial threat had to be added and it was usually only marginally effective.

The example in photo 2-16 was a coastal defence artillery firing location (Position 2, Fort Miles, Delaware) situated behind a very effectively blended transverse concrete and sand revetment. Each gun position was partially covered with netting. However, the netting was weakened as camouflage by placement against white sand that made the browns stand out (photo 2-17). Another coastal artillery battery nearby (Position 1, Fort Miles), was sited in mixed sand and scrub. Browns for camouflage worked better here (photo 2-18). A pair of overhead photos shows three stages of camouflage for the revetments and guns themselves (photos 2-19 and 2-20).

In the first photo the guns were uncamouflaged but ten tall poles can be seen bracketing the railway

2-15 Part of a German defence line in northern Europe photographed covertly in 1943, probably from a moving vehicle. The concrete was camouflaged by allowing grass to grow over much of the emplacement.

tracks just behind each weapons position. The second photo shows one revetment unoccupied and still uncamouflaged. The centre revetment had a wire framework suspended between the poles and a few panels of cloth applied. Other cloth panels were

2-16 Position 2, Fort Miles, Delaware: coastal defence railway guns behind a sand-banked transverse revetment, 16 January 1943. These gun positions would have been nearly invisible from the sea but were obvious from overhead.

draped on the revetment to disrupt its outline. The third revetment had been toned down with two colours of paint or stain added to the natural colour (compare photos). In addition, the cloth panels over the third gun position had been given a two colour random pattern.

Both of the Fort Miles batteries were rail-mounted guns with alternate sites. This meant that an enemy warship could not be sure where they were at any given time, thus the guns did not have to be as well camouflaged as permanently placed weapons. Typical of such permanent gun sites was Fort Heath, Massachusetts (photo 2-21). Located on a narrow peninsula and well known as a coastal defence position since before World War I, Fort Heath was still not easy to spot. The thick old earth and concrete escarpment shielding the guns blended well into the mottled background. From overhead, Fort Heath's camouflage gave up its secrets. The concrete gun emplacements, approach ramp and position for the optical range finder were easily seen through the camouflage netting (photo 2-22).

Another example of the sort of camouflage required for a known artillery position was that used for a German long-range gun in the 'West Wall' (photo 2-23). Heavily garnished nets were draped over the barrel and around the position itself. This passive protection may not have hidden the gun, but probably made it harder to aim at with precision from an attacking aircraft or moving warship.

Some fixed gun positions also had the flavour of mobility added to their operational capability. This apparent paradox is because the guns were on railway carriages, like the guns at Fort Miles, but the

2-17 Vertical photo of Position 2 at Fort Miles, 21 February 1943. Camouflage netting that did not match the sand was counterproductive.

guns in question were not always in place. Unlike the Fort Heath guns which were always in the area at one of their firing locations, in the late 30s it was common German and French practice to garrison their heavy rail-guns in a few central locations. Each battery was assigned a series of prepared and surveyed spurs as firing alternatives. When needed, the guns would be hauled to their widely dispersed operational positions. Once deployed, usually in pairs, the guns and crews could remain in position as long as required.

Curved sidings that led nowhere or firing turntables, (both essential for azimuth changes) were signatures for these ultra-heavy artillery positions that made them easy to identify on aerial imagery (photo 2-24). The guns in this example were German, located near Marignane in France. Their 90-foot diameter turntables were toned down to make them harder to see from the air. The guns themselves, and their ammunition cars, were under tents of netting covering the rails at key points. From a distance the firing positions were nicely hidden, but those large net awnings actually attracted attention from intelligence, rather than serving to camouflage the installation. Had the guns and ammunition been sited in holding positions some distance from the firing turntables, or under less obtrusive camouflage,

2-18 Position 1, Fort Miles, Delaware, 16 January 1943. These coastal defence railway guns were situated in terrain well suited to camouflage.

2-19 Position 1 at Fort Miles from overhead, 16 January 1943. Other than a few bushes, earthen revetments were uncamouflaged. Four poles on either side of the rails just behind the firing position were to carry netting to shield both sun and observation.

34

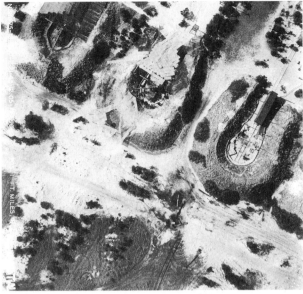

2-20 Fort Miles Position 1 after camouflage had begun, 21 February 1943. Two different schemes were used for the revetments. The centre position had cloth panels draped over the dirt and the top position had its surface stained with at least two colours. Each position had five poles on each side to hold a light mesh and two versions of coloured cloth panel camouflage were in use.

2-21 Oblique view of the Fort Heath battery showing the effectiveness of its camouflage, 10 January 1943.

these firing positions would have been more secure from detection.

Small Fixed Positions

Fixed defensive positions that were small or constructed after the war began, had the advantage of being able to remain hidden until they fired or were otherwise discovered. A few were built as concrete blockhouses and camouflaged in a cursory manner (photos 2-25 and 2-26). These were not designed to hold off heavy weapons, rather they were designed to be temporary blocks. As such, they did not have to be heavily camouflaged since once combat began their survival was brief against anything larger than normal infantry weapons. Occasionally one of these blockhouses was successfully disguised as an innocent structure (photo 2-27).

2-22 A three-gun coastal artillery battery camouflaged with earth and netting, Fort Heath, Mass., 25 February 1942. Note how the camera looks through the netting.

The ideal situation for a camouflaged blocking position was for it to be built in secret, sometimes by modifying an existing building or landform. The gun position would then remain dormant, and undiscovered, until an enemy was near. When enemy troops were in a vulnerable position, the heavily disguised gun location would drop its cover to open a devastating fire on the unsuspecting soldiers. Finding these covert gun positions was naturally a major task for photo interpreters directly supporting front-line activity.

By mid-war nearly everything intended to withstand even a minor attack was built at least partially underground (photo 2-28). Installations of this type did not require a great deal of supplemental camouflage. A few nets, some added piles of earth or a little toning down with paint served to camouflage these semi-underground positions (photos 2-29 and 2-30). The most important camouflage enhancement to defence positions developed late in the war came from discipline. First and foremost was the necessity to mask obvious scars left by construction and second was the discipline by the bunker occupants to avoid making paths that would give the bunker location away (photo 2-31).

In the Pacific, fixed defence positions of considerable strength and imaginatively camouflaged became the norm. The Japanese became masters of constructing these small defensive nodes.

2-23 Garnished netting draping a German long-range coastal gun in northern France.

2-24 (Right) British photo of a pair of 90ft-diameter turntables for super-heavy railway guns in northern France, December 1943. The guns and ammunition cars were under netting that cast strong shadows.

Most positions of this type were made with local materials. Palm logs were the most common material, but concrete, steel, and coral were also used. Most of these defences were situated to fire on beaches and were well hidden under natural camouflage materials (photo 2-32). They were disguised to blend into the debris of a jungle floor and built tough enough to withstand a considerable pounding from infantry weapons and artillery (photo 2-33).

Rear Echelon Disguise

Tactical military installations in the rear or second echelon include camps, supply dumps, headquarters and the weapons to protect them.[2] Through naiveté, ignorance, arrogance or because the troops were just plain lazy, a lot of information was given to enemy intelligence by undisguised rear echelon positions. These scraps of information were not all related to huge depots or bivouacs. They might include spotting a few tents casually situated in an olive grove behind the lines indicating military activity in the nearby buildings (photo 2-34). This, in turn, might be matched with directional fixes of communications intercepts to disclose a tactical headquarters or perhaps a better understanding of an enemy's infrastructure.

Generally speaking, in the 1930s military assets in temporary locations beyond the range of enemy guns were considered safe from observation and

---

2. Through the inter-war years, the nations that would become the Axis and the Allies each had agents, military attachés and serving officer 'tourists' going about each other's territory gathering information. A great deal of time and effort was spent, sometimes at great risk, identifying locations and functions of military installations in potential enemy countries. This resulted in a lot of information, most of which was really of little importance once a war of movement began.

2-25 British pillbox at Singapore, 1941. This defence work was painted, but poorly hidden.

2-26 German steel and concrete anti-tank position painted in an attempt to break up its outline. The round holes at left top and right side were made by US armour-piercing rounds.

2-27 A small house 'modified' to serve as a gun position. The knock-out panels were designed to look like walls until the second they fell to surprise attackers. (German, probably in Greece or southern Italy in 1944.)

destruction. Improved intelligence collection (with faster, longer-range aircraft), and better turn-around times in intelligence from collection through interpretation to use by strike aircraft, changed all that. By 1940 it was generally understood that the rear echelon had to be both defended and camouflaged. Carelessness in either category might result in the loss of a military initiative. This loss could come from the destruction of advanced headquarters or supply dumps or from a premature awareness by the enemy that an offensive was in the offing.

When the Allies were building up for the Normandy invasion, hiding the requisite depots and headquarters was a major task. It was vital that these assets not be bombed – indeed not be discovered by German intelligence. Discovery of the vast dumps of all manner of war material and numerous motor pools, troop concentrations and command posts in the south of England, instead of the east, would have broken the carefully built up deception of an Allied intent to land across the narrowest part of the Channel. This critical deception scheme was maintained through the dual techniques of active and passive defence of southern England. Active defence was in the form of fighter planes and anti-aircraft

guns denying the Luftwaffe a chance to perform aerial photoreconnaissance over the real invasion build-up areas. Passive defence was, of course, camouflage of the materiel and manpower being amassed, along with decoy dumps and camps in areas suggesting a cross-channel landing.

Huge supply dumps were covered by netting. Hundreds of miles of netting were spread over southern England, much of it rather ineptly. Typically, shadows and access roads easily gave this type of camouflage away (photo 2-35). Trucks under netting parked in towns might have made specific type identification difficult for German photo interpreters, but generic identification would have been simple (photo 2-36). Certainly German intelligence would have understood that a build-up was in progress.

A much better and more widely used camouflage technique was to put vehicles in pairs or threes under tarpaulins to mask their individual aspect ratios if they were discovered. The vehicles were then parked along field boundaries where their shadows or their bulk would not be so apparent (photo 2-37). The thickening of a hedgerow or abnormal track activity might well be missed by a careless or tired German PI. When it really mattered, the Allies could do a

2-28 German pillbox set in a roadcut and hidden with dirt and nets, southern France, 1945.

2-29 German Pz.Kpfw III tank turret set in concrete as a pillbox. The paint job was well chosen for the background.

2-30 German underground fort on the south coast of France, February 1945. The low, toned-down concrete pillboxes were also masked with netting.

2-31 German gun position in southern France camouflaged by natural growth on top and netting in front garnished with cut branches, 1945.

2-32 Palm branch camouflaged Japanese beach defence position (probably in the Philippines).

2-33 Japanese log and earth pillbox of photo 2-32 with its camouflage removed.

marvellous job of camouflage. An example was a building complex at Bushy Park, London (photo 2-38). The key structures were located under a nicely sloped umbrella of heavy netting. A few trees were allowed to rise above the cover to add authenticity.

The Bushy Park camouflage was the exception rather than the rule. Most Allied cover work was nowhere near this good. The standard of camouflage deteriorated as the Normandy landings approached, partly as a natural result of having to camouflage on such a massive scale. Another cause was that the work involved so many people over such a broad area that it was hard to maintain the highest quality work, let alone camouflage discipline. Fortunately for the Allies, the Germans never saw the inadequately camouflaged dumps and row upon row of guns and vehicles. German intelligence could

2-34 *This German camp in an olive grove showed a complete lack of camouflage discipline, Crete, 1942.*

3. Even covered tanks, guns, trucks and various stores of supplies could be identified by a PI. For vehicles, the key was to measure aspect ratios. A tank was roughly two widths long, a truck three to five widths long. For supplies, the key was the arrangement of storage. Oil drums and ammunition were stored differently but both were piled in small, well separated lots because of their hazardous nature. Boxes and crates of foodstuffs and other non-hazardous supplies were stacked in still another manner, more densely packed for ease of handling. Regardless of any specific identifications, the mass of materiel involved could only have meant an Allied invasion from ports nearest the supplies. Invasion of the continent from ports in southern England would not suggest Pas de Calais. The location of this Allied build-up made Brittany or Normandy suspect – but apparently German reconnaissance never saw it.

2-35 *Net-covered Allied depot in England, 4 December 1944. Even on small scale photography the uncamouflaged roads and shadows from entrances would betray these stacks of materiel*

2-36 US equipment hidden under nets in an English village, 30 May 1944. A German photo interpreter might have had trouble with specific identifications, but would have understood that a build-up was in progress. (DAVA-USArmy)

2-37 Tanks and half-tracks stored between a country road and hedgerow near Ashchurch, England, 10 February 1943. The tarps not only hid vehicle shapes but broke their shadows. (DAVA-USArmy)

2-38 A complete blanket of heavy netting covered a US building at Bushy Park, near London, 5 December 1943. The gentle slope and allowing trees to protrude made this work outstanding – if the entrances did not throw betraying shadows. (DAVA-USArmy)

not have mistaken the significance of such a mass of materiel along the south coast of England.[3]

Rear echelon activities in the immediate combat zone were as important as those further back in the base of operations. Some of the most critical and vulnerable rear echelon facilities just behind the battle area were refuelling points. The example shows a US Army tank farm and pump station in Normandy (photo 2-39). Not only was this facility marvellously covered with netting, but the site selection was masterful. Between two established roads, the refuelling station would not even be given away by a line of trucks on the road waiting to be loaded. The only flaw, if it can be called that, was a widening of the upper road from the beach to the inland side of the pump station.

Tactical headquarters were another type of rear echelon objective sought by cameras in the sky. When armies were on the move their command locations were always shifting. The most common disguise for such a headquarters was simply to use existing buildings for so short a time that tell-tale indicators,

2-39 US Army fuel storage and pumping station on the Normandy beachhead camouflaged with nets. Sharp eyes will spot another netted installation further up the road, 3 October 1944. (DAVA-USArmy)

2-40 A German field headquarters in Pas-de-Calais, near Montreuil, France exercised good camouflage discipline in the placement of its vehicle park. It was located when British photoreconnaissance caught an Hs 126 army co-operation plane landing, June 1940.

like track activity, did not build up. All that was necessary on the ground was to ensure that the numerous vehicles always present at headquarters did not show on enemy aerial photography. During their advance in 1940, the Germans followed all the camouflage discipline rules at a tactical command position near Montreuil, France. Their vehicle park was well hidden in a tree line and track activity was nothing unusual for a group of farm buildings. This German position might well have escaped detection for some time but British Intelligence had a bit of luck when their photo reconnaissance caught a German Hs 126 army co-operation plane on the ground (photo 2-40). The aircraft was taxying towards the farm buildings. Once attention was called to the area the carefully parked vehicles were spotted, giving this location away as the temporary headquarters of a senior army element.

Rear echelon defence was also an active subject for camoufleurs, especially so if the military asset to be defended was very likely to be attacked from the air. One of the more imaginative camouflage jobs on a defence position in the rear echelon was the use of fake tents to mask anti-aircraft machine guns (photo 2-41). These were developed by the British in Libya and served to hide guns while still permitting them to come into action quickly (photo 2-42).

In the early days of war, before radar controlled AA guns and night-fighters, one of the main weapons against night bombers was the searchlight. If the lights could catch a bomber, then the gunners could have a go at it. This in turn made searchlights a target in their own right. Enemy intelligence always knew just where to look for searchlights – they had to be near the guns. The characteristic large round shape of the lights made them easy to locate in both direct viewing or by their shadow. Because of this, special camouflage treatment was required to hide these fragile assets (photo 2-43).

Special and Unusual

Radio and radar antennas were both hard to disguise and vulnerable to attack. On the other hand, many antennas were small in size or made of open

meshwork and therefore hard to see from the air. If an antenna could be spotted and identified from the air, the associated functions being performed nearby would also be identified. This could give away the location of headquarters, air controller positions or early-warning networks.

On rocky Canton Island a US radar was camouflaged by a canvas cover painted to match the small mottled pattern of the ground (photo 2-44). The

2-41 Camouflage cover for an anti-aircraft machine gun position in a tent area, Benghazi Camp site, Libya, 9 September 1943. (DAVA-USArmy)

2-42 The fake tent of photo 2-41 could be quickly opened to get the gun into action. (DAVA-USArmy)

4. In 1942, Canton Island was thought in danger from Japanese aerial attack or shelling from a submarine. Thus this camouflage was oriented to horizontal as well as vertical observation. The Tonga Islands, south of Samoa, might only be attacked from the sea by 1944 – and that was unlikely.

2-43 A camouflaged searchlight during US Army manoeuvres in the Carolinas, November 1941. The canvas tarp and drape of netting garnished with branches were intended to alter the characteristic shape and shadow of the light. (National Archives)

2-44 A US radar hidden by a canvas cover painted to blend into the barren landscape of Canton Island, July 1942.

antenna itself was painted a light colour to blend with the sky when viewed horizontally.[4] The control van of an American SCR270 radar on Tonga Island was disguised as a native hut (photo 2-45). The antenna itself was left in the open.

Characteristic shadows could give antennas away, so provisions were taken to radically alter the appearance of antennas when enemy planes were active in an area. A good example of this was at Hitler's retreat near Berchtesgaden, Germany (photo 2-46). These radio antennas were draped with garnished netting to make them appear as trees. Comparison with the men or nearby buildings will give some idea of the size of these radio antennas.

Another group of targets every bit as characteristic in shape as antennas was the German V-1, flying bomb, launch sites. When first discovered, these positions were located just inland from the coast of north-western France, threatening England. The V-1 sites were made up of various control buildings, a launching ramp and three missile assembly and check-out buildings. The latter were the real keys, or signatures, of the sites since their unusual curved entrances were unlike anything else. These buildings looked like skis lying on their side, so the V-1 launch complexes soon became known as 'ski-sites'. Most of the early V-1 launch sites were located for operational reasons, such as a clear line of fire. This put many of them pretty much out in the open.

To pinpoint the launch sites, Allied photo interpreters had only to scan area coverage imagery for the characteristic ski-shape. The Germans quickly understood the signature value of the ski-shapes and sought to disguise them. At Bois Carre, false roofing was added to convert the ski buildings into more innocent appearing structures (photo 2-47). Allied intelligence was not fooled.[5]

---

5 The Bois Carre V-1 launch site near Yvrench, France, was the first one known to the Allies. An agent's report in October 1943 originally called British Intelligence's attention to the site. Bois Carre was photo-confirmed as a V-1 launch position in early November. Once they knew what to look for, 96 of the 'ski-sites' were located by photo interpreters within two months.

More effective camouflage of the V-1 sites was achieved by carefully placing the characteristic structures where their lines would not be so apparent (photo 2-48). Camouflage was then added and camouflage discipline was excellent. This made the Allied photo interpretation task considerably more difficult. Finding the ski-sites became a matter of having photoreconnaissance pilots fly dangerous area-coverage missions. Allied PIs would then laboriously scan every inch of every frame of photography.[6] Had it not been for the Allied command of the air allowing the entire V-1 launch zone to be covered by photoreconnaissance, the excellent German positioning of launch sites would have insured the survival of many of these lethal weapons. Given sufficient priority, blanket aerial photo cover and enough PIs – all of which this task had – there was no way that the ski-sites could escape detection.[7]

Armies on the Move

Armies on the march were unusually visible and terribly vulnerable to aerial observation and air attack. Despite mobile AA guns travelling with the army columns, it was one of those cases where there was no really good solution – just the hope of making the best of a bad situation. The hope was that the moving force would not be seen and caught from the air. The most common response to this camouflage problem was to simply cut brush or branches and tie them on equipment (photo 2-49). The object was to pull in close to a tree line if an enemy aircraft was heard. Snuggling next to tree lines or hedgerows was an effective defence against being seen from the air if track activity did not give the location away (photo 2-50).

Forces on the move were always careful to camouflage equipment parked for the night or even for a meal stop (photo 2-51). The example, from the German advance into the Soviet Union in 1941, shows vehicles and trailers carefully hidden in a Russian farmyard.

Tactical Positions

Front-line positions were more difficult to camouflage than most because they always had to be

2-45 The control van of an American SCR270 radar disguised as a native hut, Tonga Islands, 1944.

proofed against horizontal as well as aerial observation. On the plus side, the groups of men and equipment to be hidden were usually smaller than those to be hidden in the second echelon. This also made them easier to camouflage. The camouflage was usually ad hoc, making heavy use of materials at hand. In the brush country of the Philippines, freshly cut branches made a good disguise for an anti-tank gun (photo 2-52).

Camouflage discipline was essential for lightly covered tactical positions (photo 2-53). In this example, from an exercise in Louisiana, nicely hidden anti-tank guns were disclosed by a carelessly positioned, uncamouflaged radio truck.

Even worse than poor camouflage discipline was selection of camouflage materials that did not blend into the surrounding ground. A US Army 105mm howitzer was a big object to hide behind a few scraggly branches (photo 2-54). A 'better than nothing' philosophy probably motivated this gun crew, photographed during manoeuvres in California in 1942. Actually, a lighter colour paint on the gun and some digging-in would have been a better solution to this camouflage problem.

With natural vegetation at a minimum, camouflage

---

6. Area coverage photo missions over hostile territory were unusually hazardous because they involved long legs of straight and level flight at medium altitudes. Because these flight legs were predictable, the mission aircraft were vulnerable to interception. Every photo was carefully examined for signs of the ski buildings. Very quickly the zone where V-1 launch sites were being found narrowed to a strip of France 10-30 miles from the coast between the Seine and the Belgian border. Every inch of every previous photo taken in the suspect area was looked at again and again in the search for the signature ski-shaped buildings that gave away these sites.

7. By February 1944 the Germans also recognised that the ski-shaped buildings were a signature for V-1 launch sites. The next generation of launch sites were made without the ski buildings. The photo search began all over again and this time the targets were smaller. By April 1944, 68 of the abbreviated, less obvious V-1 sites had been found through a massive and thorough PI screening effort. Finding and destroying V-1 sites was the highest priority at the time because these weapons were a serious threat to the Normandy invasion ports in southern England.

Above and Above Right: 2-46 German radio antennas disguised as trees, Berchtesgaden, Germany, 1945.

Right: 2-47 German V-1 launch site in Normandy, January 1944. The characteristic flat-roofed buildings were being camouflaged with fake peaked roofs. Some roof frames can be seen on the ground.

Below Right: 2-48 As the Allies got better at finding V-1 sites in Normandy, the Germans got better at hiding them; 31 December 1943. Can you find the three ski-shaped assembly buildings and launching ramp? (see Appendix II for the solution)

in the desert was a real art, but it could be mastered (photo 2-55). By 1943, US troops were learning to use natural cover effectively. The example photo was taken during a US Army desert manoeuvre and covers a position with vehicles, field guns and over 100 men. Not only was the use of available cover excellent, but only a few men broke cover to gawk at the low flying photo plane.

Sometimes the available cover was more important for its pattern than for its shield value. In the case of an anti-aircraft battery, the guns had to be able to sweep the sky to track targets. Obviously these guns could not be under tangles of nets. A four-gun mobile heavy anti-aircraft battery in training in England was effectively disguised by mimicking the square shapes of the surrounding housing blocks (photo 2-56).

2-49 Soviet 152mm howitzer on the move camouflaged with branches, during the German invasion of Russia in 1941.

A pair of German light anti-aircraft batteries tried to pose as hayricks in the Netherlands in late 1944 (photo 2-57). The gun positions were carefully located in several fields and special attention was clearly taken to avoid tell-tale track activity. These casual dots on the ground might have escaped attention had it not been for the diligence of an Allied photo interpreter – and comparative photo cover. Scanning frame after frame of photography covering routine countryside was one of the most demanding and boring tasks in the intelligence business. It was also one of the most important. It is easy to look for and interpret installations that are already known, the hard part is to find new ones. In this case, the PI found those seven tiny dots through a millimeter-by-millimeter search of his photography compared with that of the preceding day (photo 2-58).

Dummies

Decoys and dummies were often used because they drew fire or made it appear that a force was larger than it really was. Dummy positions could also be used to mask a troop withdrawal. One such use of dummy troops and fake guns was at Cape Gloucester, on the western tip of New Britain Island, in December 1943 (photo 2-59). These gun positions had a ring of authenticity (proper tracks and trash) because at one time they had housed real guns. The nature of the dummies was given away when 'the troops' didn't duck for cover as bombs went off. A typical dummy gun position consisted of an old uniform stuffed with straw behind a wooden gun (photo 2-60). Close inspection easily revealed this type of deception but the set-up cost was low, and a fast moving strafer might be fooled.

Dummies of large guns, such as field artillery, were intended to fool ground as well as aerial attackers (photo 2-61). Once again the construction material

2-50 The most basic form of camouflage from aerial observation: staying next to a tree line. Careless exposure of tracks would lead a photo interpreter to the equipment, Normandy, 7 June 1944.

2-51 German photo of trucks and trailers camouflaged with branches and well situated against farm buildings, near Pomeran'ye in the Soviet Union, 28 April 1942.

2-52 Cut branches used to camouflage a US Army 37mm anti-tank gun in the Philippines, 24 July 1941. (DAVA-USArmy)

2-53 Camouflage discipline was essential. Nicely hidden anti-tank guns on the right were given away by the nearby radio truck parked in the open. US Army manoeuvres, Camp Polk, La., 12 February 1943. (DAVA-USArmy)

2-54 Cut brush camouflage for a US Army 105mm Howitzer during desert manoeuvres, September 1942. The gun and branches were totally out of place in these surroundings. (DAVA-USArmy)

was usually wood and the design ad hoc. The work involved was generally just enough to suggest the point. This lack of detail was the surest key for enemy intelligence to quickly pick out fakes. Dummy positions were sometimes simply painted on the ground or lightly marked with stones. Troops seldom wanted to go to the trouble of digging revetments that would never be used as revetments (photo 2-62). Another intelligence tip-off of a decoy was the lack of clutter and track activity always present at a real installation (photo 2-63). Unless the NCOs stood by strict camouflage discipline, troops would always take the shortest route between their position and the latrine or mess.

The warring armies all spent a great deal of time,

money and effort exploring better and more convincing ways to deceive each other. One of the biggest deception programmes was operated by the US Army Corps of Engineers with much of their work being done at Fort Belvoir, Va, just south of Washington DC. There the engineers tried a variety of schemes ranging from valuable to strange. Among the camouflage and deception techniques developed were fake trees that troops could make from empty ration tins and a full range of dummy vehicles. One of the most unusual camouflage techniques was the painting of trucks and tanks on the floor of a landing craft (photo 2-64).

More successful, and certainly of great use, were the experiments conducted to develop highly

2-55 *Excellent use of natural and artificial cover during US Army desert manoeuvres at Camp Young, Cal., 15 January 1943. There are trucks, artillery pieces and over 100 men on this photo (arrows indicate typical positions). The tailless arrow shows the only men who broke cover when the reconnaissance plane overflew the area.*

realistic three-dimensional inflated rubber dummy vehicles and weapons (photo 2-65). The example shows real and inflated vehicles photographed together from an altitude of 1,000 feet. Even from that close it is hard to pick out the fakes. Rubber dummies such as these were expected to play a significant role in the huge deception scheme masking the Normandy invasion. Large numbers of fake landing craft were positioned along the English coast opposite Pas de Calais to convince Hitler that it was there that the Allies would strike (photos 2-66 and 2-67). The woods of Kent and East Anglia were studded with fake campsites and equipment such as heavy artillery pieces and tanks (photos 2-68 and 2-69). These dummies helped simulate an Allied army that didn't exist.[8] The unusually elaborate rubber dummies were carefully positioned to appear as though they were ineptly hidden. The RAF permitted a few Luftwaffe reconnaissance planes through to ensure that German intelligence got the message.[9]

On the far side of the world decoy/dummy production was far less organised. The Japanese produced a large number of land warfare decoys, but most of them were so naively designed and executed as to be useless (photo 2-70). A few involved so much work, yet were so ridiculous, that their intent is hard to understand (photo 2-71).

Few tactical decoys or camouflage jobs fooled anyone very long. However, given the highly transitory nature of land war, fooling an enemy for a

2-56 *A four-gun anti-aircraft artillery position in England hidden by copying local rectangular patterns, August 1943.*

few hours or days was often enough to help real assets or intentions survive.

---

8. Huge and elaborate decoy and deception operations were mounted to simulate a large Allied force poised to leap directly across the English Channel. Acres of empty tents, dummy weapons, vehicles and landing craft, and fake supply dumps supported flurries of bogus radio traffic between non-existent units. With great publicity, Lt.-Gen. George S. Patton, Jr. was pulled from the war in Italy and put in charge of the US Third Army in England. The Germans did what they were supposed to do by concluding that Patton – a combat commander they knew and respected – would lead the Allied cross-channel invasion. At this point in time, Patton's Third Army, its divisions and all its equipment in East Anglia were entirely fictional.

9. The RAF had successfully frozen Luftwaffe daylight reconnaissance planes out of southern England since late 1942. To enhance the deception of a cross-channel landing in 1944, the Allies permitted a few German sorties into Kent and East Anglia while blocking similar flights over the actual invasion build up area. The Luftwaffe planes were supposed to photograph the large collection of decoys, thereby lending credence to other deceptions suggesting a massive build up. If the US collection of captured German aerial photography is comprehensive, all of this effort was apparently wasted. I have not been able to find a single example of a German intelligence aerial photo of the Allied decoy/deception installations.

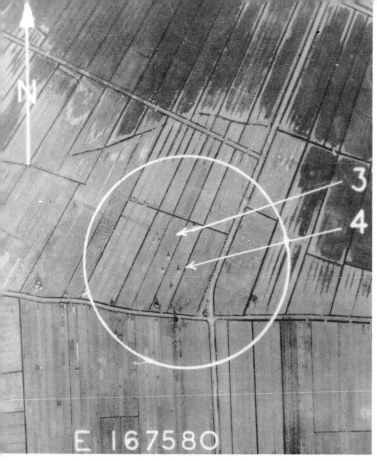

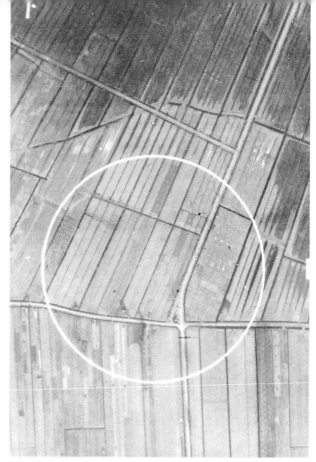

2-57 Sharp-eyed British photo interpreters found these German anti-aircraft guns situated unobtrusively in open fields, Netherlands, 26 December 1944.

2-58 The key to success in photo 2-57 – photography of the same area one day earlier. Comparative aerial photo coverage could defeat almost any camouflage.

2-59 Japanese decoy artillery position, Cape Gloucester, New Britain Island in the Bismarcks. Real troops would be ducking from the exploding bombs.

2-60 Dummy anti-aircraft machine-gun position at an Allied airfield in India, 1943.

DUMMY F.A. POSITION

F.A. REPORT NO. 5

Location: Map Ref. GSGS 4250, Sheet 16 NE
         Coord. 974289
Sortie : 4/117, Photos 4007-8

Dummy FA positions are often used by the Germans to mislead AOP and FO. Unless they are elaborately constructed, however, they will seldom fool a photo interpreter. Lack of shadow, lack of track activity, lack of depth quickly give them away.

This dummy position might have been built to protect the battery reported on in FA report No. 1. Construction is evident from the ground photos.

The four positions along the hedgerow are four more dummy positions constructed in a similar manner. Notice in each case that the Germans were careful to simulate foxholes and trenches, but the lack of depth and the obviousness of the battery when compared with an actual battery position makes it easy to spot as a dummy. It lacks finesse. A dummy to be successful must recieve a great deal of careful attention.

Fig. No. 1 Typical dummy field gun

Fig. No. 2 Typical dummy battery

One interpreter reports: "Dummy batteries have always proven interesting because Jerry is admitting that he's aware of our PI's. By ground checking, we're able to keep score, matching our interpretations against his ingenuity. The Germans, up to the time of the December 17 counteroffensive, appeared to be using dummies in increasing numbers. Admitting that dummy batteries are hard to distinguish from real ones, there are certain tips that might be of some aid to interpreters in making differentiation. First, all dummy batteries were in open fields; secondly, there is usually an absence of track activity; thirdly, whereas around the real batteries there are numerous deeply-dug shelters and storage trenches, the 'trenches' are mere scratches on the ground around dummy batteries. Thus there will be deep shadows in the trenches in the vicinity of real batteries and an absence of shadows around dummies."

Fig. No. 3 Dummy 88mm. gun

2-62 Page from a US report on German artillery dummies, early 1945.

2-61 Page from a British report on a dummy field artillery position. This site was betrayed by its lack of three-dimensional construction and track activity.

2-63 Anti-aircraft artillery position on Haines Point, Washington DC, 6 July 1942. The absence of beaten paths going to the 'guns' disclosed this as a dummy.

2-64 *An LCT with a painted load, Fort Belvoir, Va, 1 May 1944.*

2-65 *Real and inflated rubber dummy vehicles in a US Army Engineer test, Fort Belvoir, Va., 7 July 1944. See Appendix II for the key to which are real and which are decoys.*

2-66 (Top) An exact full-scale inflated rubber replica of a US LCT being unpacked by sailors and engineers. (DAVA-US Army)

2-67 (Above) Fully inflated dummy LCT afloat with its ramp realistically open. (DAVA-US Army)

2-68 (Right) Highly detailed, inflated rubber US 155mm 'Long Tom' weighing 250 lbs. Dummies like this were used as part of a massive deception effort to mask the Normandy Invasion in June 1944. (DAVA-US Army)

2-69 Inflated dummy US 'Sherman' tank with realistic painting to add to its effectiveness, England, 1944. (DAVA-USArmy)

2-70 A sheet-metal and wood tank dummy made by the Japanese in Burma, May 1945. It is doubtful if anyone would go for this decoy.

2-71 The ultimate in immobile decoys, a Japanese tank made of mud bricks, Yenangyaung oil fields, Burma, May 1945.

CHAPTER 3

PAINT DOESN'T STICK ON WATER
Camouflaging Naval and Marine Targets

Naval targets were among the most difficult to hide from searching bomber crews and intelligence analysts and among the most satisfying for analysts to find. Given a reasonably good photo, and armed with detailed reference books, a PI could usually identify a major naval or commercial vessel down to the ship name – thus exposing all the type, speed, firepower, carrying-capacity etc.

Everyone knew enemy naval units had to be on water, therefore all the major bays, rivers and ports had been minutely mapped for over a century. To make matters more complicated for a defender, it is virtually impossible to camouflage an ocean.

On the other hand, there are hundreds of thousands of miles of coast and three-fourths of the world is water; that gave plenty of room in which to hide. The hiding was facilitated if a ship could be made to blend with the sea or a shore background.

Ideally, intelligence would have found enemy ships at sea just like targets were found on the land. Over time, huge areas of open water would have been covered by small-scale aerial photography that photo interpreters would scan in detail to locate and identify any naval units present. However, ships, unlike their support facilities, did not remain in the same place. In any case, no World War II reconnaissance plane could carry enough film to conduct really effective blanket photo surveillance flights over land, let alone the ocean. Ships at sea or hiding along shorelines, had to be found by surface observation, visual reconnaissance from the air, or through tips from communications intelligence. The suspected areas or vessels thus located could then be photographed for positive ship identification.

Even with these techniques, finding a moving ship at sea was somewhat a matter of chance. An enemy ship had to be using its radios or the opposing reconnaissance aircraft had to be at the right place at the right time. If a plane was high enough and properly positioned, weather permitting, ship wakes could be seen at surprisingly great distances. The faster a ship was moving, then the greater this acquisition distance would be (photo 3-1). For example, US aircraft patrolling north of Guadalcanal at around 18,000 feet altitude routinely spotted Japanese destroyers eight to ten miles away.[1] Sighting fast moving warships at even greater distances was not uncommon.

Ship Camouflage

Both sides in the war understood that if an enemy plane happened to be in the right location it was impossible to hide moving ships from aerial observation. Therefore, individual ships were camouflaged with the same logic used to hide land assets in a tactical environment. They were disguised either to blend into their background or to alter their signature characteristics. The best they could hope for was to confuse or delay detection and identification by an enemy.

A vessel such as a Patrol Torpedo-boat was commonly based at austere facilities near the front. Underway, a PT-boat survived because of its speed and manoeuvrability. A PT operated short sorties, frequently at night, and was extremely vulnerable to air attack while tied up during the day.

Unless it could be placed in a bomb-proof shelter, it was natural to camouflage such a warship to blend into its berthing environment.[2] In the Pacific it was common to paint PT-boats to blend into a jungle background (photo 3-2).[3] The subdued contrast between bands of different earth or foliage colours would be dark enough to provide cover while underway at night and would afford good visual cover in the poor light of dawn or dusk. Regardless of any advantage this camouflage scheme might have at sea, its main function was day camouflage against surface and low-flying aerial observation while the PT-boat lay against a jungle shore.

Transports and cargo ships were large vessels that spent most of their time in major ports where disguise was either unnecessary or ineffective. At sea their voyages were long and relatively slow and they were extremely vulnerable if discovered. Commercial ships had neither the speed, manoeuvrability nor weapons to protect themselves, so their camouflage was designed to avoid detection at sea for as long as possible. They were painted to blend into the seascape, using neutral blues, greys and sea-greens (photo 3-3). Compare the two passenger liners with dulled paint

---

1. These were five ships of Rear-Admiral Tanaka's 'Tokyo Express' heading down 'The Slot' from the Shortlands to Guadalcanal.

2. Care had to be taken to insure that land-oriented camouflage did not make the Patrol Torpedo-boat more conspicuous on the ocean.
3. This US PT-boat was under tow when photographed by a US reconnaissance plane.

schemes to the background ship which still carries a peacetime black and white paint designed to make it stand out against the sea.[4]

Warship camouflage was different from that used on commercial ships because warships had a different reason for being on the broad ocean and a different mode of operation. Large combat vessels often spent very long periods at sea, but, while not seeking enemy detection, they were not out there to shun contact. Most commonly, warships were painted to spoil the attack of an enemy ship or plane. For this reason they were most often camouflaged to confuse or delay enemy firing. The same dull colours used on more passive ships were employed but they were often supplemented with sharply contrasting dark or light colours applied to disrupt the ship's outline. This painted disruption might at times also make the ships harder to see, but its primary purpose was to make the ship type harder to identify. Also, if applied correctly, disruptive paint could for a short time deny an enemy airman, submariner or gunner one or more of the critical attack factors; ship speed, direction of movement and distance.

The Home Fleet ferry service carrier HMS *Fencer*[5] was painted in an updated version of World War I dazzle paint (photo 3-4). Further away on the same photo a larger carrier, HMS *Furious*, shows a paint job designed to hide the flight deck. Large dark patches fore-and-aft of a normal superstructure position tend to make the carrier's outline appear as a conventional warship.[6] A third ship, apparently also an aircraft carrier, had an outline so disrupted by its camouflage that it cannot be positively identified from this photo.

Irregular patches of dull coloured paint do not necessarily make good camouflage. A three-colour

Top: 3-1 Japanese destroyer wakes at better than 8 miles. North-west of Guadalcanal, 26 October 1942.

Above: 3-2 A jungle-blending disruptive paint pattern on a US PT-boat in the south-west Pacific, 1 August 1943.

disruptive pattern was used on the British battleship HMS *Nelson* in 1943–44 (photo 3-5). The paint did not particularly hide or confuse the ship's outline nor alter its apparent size. While possibly of some help in making the battleship blend into a sea background, the camouflage cannot be classed as very effective. Conversely, the same photo shows the massive bulk of a fleet-sized aircraft carrier wearing a reasonably effective three-colour scheme. The carrier's island is disguised by a large dark patch arching up to break the flat line of the flight deck. An aircraft carrier's huge and distinctive shape could not be hidden for long, but this example might confuse a distant enemy for at least a short while.[7]

Disruptive paint work was sometimes so good it even worked in port, although it was not designed

---

4. According to the 14th Squadron caption, these ships are from the 'Third Convoy'.

5. Ex-USS *Croatan*.

6. HMS *Fencer* was launched in May 1942; by that time HMS *Courageous* and HMS *Glorious* had been sunk, so the big carrier has to be HMS *Furious*. What appears to be a third carrier at rear right may be HMS *Argus*. All three carriers were with the British Home Fleet at the same time in 1943–44.

7. The futility of trying to hide a really big ship at sea was recognised after the first year of war in the Pacific but the US Navy refused to abandon disruptive camouflage for capital ships. Camouflage was not universal however, sometimes major ships were painted a solid dull blue-grey to let them blend into a basic sea background. It didn't disguise their shape but it made them harder to see.

3-3 Troopships were often painted dull grey to blend into the sea. Photo taken near Freemantle, Australia, 12 May 1940. Compare with the peace-time paint scheme in the background.

3-4 British aircraft carriers HMS Fencer and HMS Furious (background) in the Atlantic with disruptive paint work, 1943.

3-5 British battleship HMS Nelson and a carrier of the Illustrious class, probably 1943. HMS Nelson's camouflage was of questionable effectiveness, but the carrier's paint job might hide its characteristic shape for a few critical moments.

3-6 *Disruptive paint patterns could disguise the outline of a ship even in port.*

3-7 *British destroyer HMS* Javelin *painted to appear shorter to upset enemy gun-aimers' ranging.*

3-8 *A ship's speed was deceiving with a painted bow wave. US heavy cruiser USS* Salt Lake City, *1942.*

3-9 *The US heavy cruiser USS* Northampton *had a painted bow wave, but she also had her foretop works painted light grey to help obscure ship identification and make her hard to see near the horizon.*

3-10 Old style dazzle paint, or recognition stripes, on the foredecks of an Italian cruiser, destroyer and freighters, Messina, 26 August 1942.

for this effect.[8] You have to look twice to trace the ship's outline against its background in photo 3-6. Note how it is difficult to see the after limits of the ship and how its deck configuration is obscured. These were the very factors that were essential in engaging a ship at sea. If the type and class of an enemy ship could be identified, its known size could be compared to the length observed to precisely determine how far away it was. Type and class identification were also vital to knowing what weapons an adversary could bring into the fight. Camouflage served its purpose if it first made a

ship harder to acquire visually, then added a few moments of confusion as to type, class, speed or range. Even a momentary confusion by enemy gunners might improve ones chances to get off the first shot.

Painted Trickery

Range was so important to the gunnery equation that special camouflage efforts were often made purely to deny an enemy this data. One such attempt was on the British destroyer HMS *Javelin*.[9] The ship was painted to appear shorter than it actually was (photo 3-7). This would give the

---

8. Photo 3-6 is undated but captioned HMAS *Athenia*. I cannot find a record of a ship by that name, but the vessel is similar in configuration to USS *Athene*, a merchant ship converted to an aircraft transporter.

9. One of HMS *Javelin*'s sister ships was HMS *Kelly*, Earl Mountbatten's ship that sank under him in the Mediterranean on 22 May 1941.

3-11 Disruptive paint could not hide the Japanese carrier Zuiho *off the Philippines Cape Engano in late October 1944.*

impression of *Javelin* being either a much smaller ship or a ship much further away. In either case, enemy pilots or gunners would have difficulty ranging the target.

Other critical factors in accurate naval target engagement were the speed and direction of travel of the attack objective. Ship speed could be confused by a painted bow wave, as on the US heavy cruiser USS *Salt Lake City* (photo 3-8). This tended to make the ship look as though it was cutting through the water at a good clip regardless of its actual speed. Estimating a ship's speed as higher than it actually was, along with observing its actual horizontal movement, added confusion on course and distance calculations. This could lead an enemy to think the ship was further away or that its course was angling away rather than running parallel to the attacker's course. This, in turn would result in bad range prediction or too long a lead when firing.

The US heavy cruiser USS *Northampton* also sported a painted bow wave, but she showed another camouflage trick by having her upper works painted to blend into the sky. The ship herself was painted a flat dark grey to blend with the sea, but the foremast above the bridge was a light grey (photo 3-9). This would make the cruiser harder to acquire at long range, as the tall mast was made harder to see against the sky. It also tended to hide her class by confusing the cruiser's outline.[10]

Obviously not all attacks on ships would be made from the surface or by aircraft near the surface, and disguising a ship from a high-angle aerial attack was a much different problem. Most camouflage efforts against overhead observation ranged from marginally effective to ridiculous. Among the

ineffectual was Italian navy diagonal striping (photo 3-10). Ranking more as decoration than a disguise, this pattern was apparently something of a local Italian standard. It occurred on a cruiser, a destroyer and two freighters at Messina in August 1942. Always on the fore-deck, the stripes do not interrupt the ship's outline. In fact, this pattern is so useless as a ship disguise or confusion device that it is possible it was not camouflage at all. It may have been a convoy recognition pattern, much like the black and white Normandy invasion stripes on Allied aircraft in June 1944.

In October 1944 the Japanese aircraft carrier *Zuiho* exhibited a laboriously painted and totally ineffective paint pattern (photo 3-11). Disruptive shapes covered the flight deck, but any camouflage utility they might have had was destroyed by broad straight stripes and an alternating light-dark pattern on the aft end of the deck.[11] It is doubtful that this pattern achieved any camouflage effect except perhaps under netting when the carrier was in a disguised berth (photo 3-26). The camouflage certainly did not help *Zuiho* this day. At the time of the photo this carrier had taken at least three bomb hits and a section of her armoured deck was buckled from a torpedo hit just aft of mid-ships.

Paint alone could sometimes be temporarily effective to protect a warship from bombing while in port (photo 3-12). The simple act of darkening the German heavy cruiser *Hipper* made her hard to see at Kiel when bomb damage had dulled and darkened her surroundings. A combination of weak winter light and the darkening even made *Hipper* hard to identify on reconnaissance imagery.[12] It was common for both sides to paint North Atlantic ships dark grey on any surface seen from above and a lighter grey on surfaces seen from the side.

Hiding Ships

Attempting to hide a moving ship on the open sea from air identification and attack was largely a waste of time but disguising a stationary ship was sometimes relatively effective. It was equally important to insure that the vessel did not stand out from its environment as it was to camouflage the ship itself (photo 3-13).

In the South-west Pacific, thoroughly covered Japanese barges were commonly located by Allied airmen because their outlines did not merge effectively into the shoreline. The most typical camouflage used in the Pacific was simply a draping of cut branches. The price of ineffective camouflage was usually paid quickly as hunting tactical aircraft roamed the Solomons, Bismarcks,

---

10. Also note that *Northampton*'s scout planes are painted the same sky-blending light grey.

11. *Zuiho* was sunk off Cape Engano, Philippines, on 25 October 1944, shortly after this photo was taken. Some post-war works have referred to this paint job as an attempt to make the carrier look as though it had turrets. This makes no sense because US airmen knew Japan had no ship with four guns in its main turrets and disguising a carrier as a battleship would hardly afford much protection.

12. With only seconds to find the ship, aim and bomb, it is doubtful if Allied airmen could zero in on a ship so ill-defined.

3-12 German Cruiser Hipper *darkened to hide at Kiel, Germany, 22 March 1945.*

3-13 Well camouflaged but poorly positioned Japanese barges. Hanish Harbor, New Guinea, 30 July 1943.

and the New Guinea coast (photo 3-14). In this case the camouflage was netting garnished with recently cut natural vegetation.

Good individual camouflage work could be easily betrayed by less thorough efforts that called attention to an area. For example, thirteen well-covered and well-sited Japanese barges were given away by one sticking out too far from the shore and six beached beyond the tree overhang line (photo 3-15). The two nearest photo bottom were not only very poorly positioned, but were the most poorly covered with natural vegetation.[13]

Even excellent camouflage and positioning would usually fall prey to a photo interpreter using stereo viewing for a detailed examination of every inch of shoreline (photo 3-16). The Japanese barges in this photo would probably have escaped detection by a pilot with only a few seconds to spot them. However, if these barges had remained in place for several days without new branches being applied, the natural camouflage would wither and change colour. This would call a pilot's attention to the spot and the barges would be found easily.

Nets

In areas where natural camouflage material was not as abundant as it was in the South Pacific, or not as appropriate – as in a more urban area – anti-aerial camouflage was often accomplished with the use of nets. Nets tended to obscure objects from planes overhead and could also be used to blend a target into its environment. They were less effective as a

---

13. Either there are a number of barges beyond the top of the photo or the bomb from the B-26 that took the photo is going to overshoot the target by a considerable margin.

mask from intelligence collection since aerial cameras generally looked right through the camouflage netting. As an example, intelligence photography of the German port at Gdynia, Poland, could be used to count submarines seen through the nets (photo 3-17). Plain nets such as these, were even more transparent when a photo interpreter used stereo viewing. The nets used in this example were simply an open-weave fabric without paint or garnish materials.

A more important purpose for nets was to break up a ship's outline to cloud its identity from opposing intelligence. Unless the associated ship's shadows were covered up, hiding the outline was useless. Netting tended to effectively disrupt the outlines of the German battleship *Gneisenau* in dry-dock at Brest, France in 1941 (photo 3-18). But the ship's shadow showed up clearly on reconnaissance photos – and the location of the dry-dock was well known –making this net camouflage a waste of time.[14] The netting used by the Germans at Brest was once again just plain material, more like muslin than a net.

Similar netting on sister ship *Scharnhorst* at

quayside was also of little value. Even though the hull shadow did not show on the water, her superstructure shadow showed clearly. A more valuable camouflage was the fore and aft placement of floating material to help break up the overall ship outline. Had nets covered the remaining gaps between ship and quay, this camouflage would have hindered locating the battleship for precision bombing, especially at night when the RAF tended to attack.[15]

The Soviets used floating material on barges along with nets to obscure big river steamers at Sevastopol in 1942 (photo 3-19). This netting was garnished by pieces of cloth to add more density and break up the shapes and shadows underneath. German dive-bomber attention on nearby forts, rather than their camouflage, probably saved these ships which were eventually captured by the Nazis. The Soviet nets appear to be fairly effective in easing the high straight lines of the ships – but are not very good camouflage for the ships in their present position. This is a case where the camouflage would actually call attention to the two ships. They were berthed in a narrow finger of the

---

14. *Gneisenau* could have been roughly identified by Allied intelligence on her measurements alone even if she had been far more thoroughly draped with netting. *Scharnhorst* and *Gneisenau* were considered battleships by the German Navy and so carried in *Janes Fighting Ships,* but were regarded by the Royal Navy as Battlecruisers.

15. Only German flak and fighters and British difficulty in hitting such small targets, saved the two battleships (despite some damage) for nearly a year. On 11–13 February 1943 *Scharnhorst, Gneisenau* and heavy cruiser *Prinz Eugen,* covered by bad weather and massive Luftwaffe support, boldly ran from Brest to Kiel, Germany, via the Dover Straits.

3-14 The price of poor camouflage. Rein Bay, New Guinea, 9 November 1943.

3-15 Well camouflaged and well situated Japanese barges were given away to US B-26s by their poorly positioned neighbours. Borgen Bay, Bismarcks, 29 July 1943.

3-16 Extremely well-hidden Japanese barges at Rekata Bay, Solomons, found by a US photo interpreter, 8 August 1943.

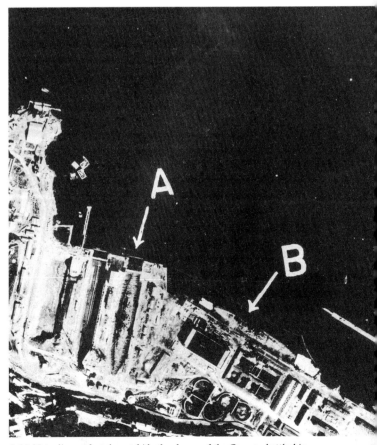

3-17 German submarines at Gdynia, Poland, 15 December 1944. The camera 'sees' through the covering nets.

3-18 Nets disrupt but do not hide the shapes of the German battleship Gneisenau (in dry-dock) or sister ship Scharnhorst (annotation B) at quayside. Brest, France, 28 May 1941.

3-19 Soviet river steamers or ferry boats hidden under disruptive netting. Sevastopol, Crimea, May 1943.

harbour[16] and had a number of smaller, undisguised vessels next to them. Finally, the effect of the nets might blend well with vegetation along a river bank in the countryside, but it was badly out of step with the clearly urban context of this port.

A better example of the use of nets and floating material to tie a ship into a shore pattern is the German light cruiser *Köln* in Foetten Fjord in 1942 (photo 3-20). In this case the remote location added to the difficulty in finding this ship, demanding either luck or comprehensive aerial photo coverage of a considerable stretch of the Norwegian coast. The cruiser herself was not camouflaged in any way.[17] This was to be expected of a ship that might have to sortie quickly. Encumbering camouflage that had to be cleared off to get underway would degrade the cruiser's operational status. With a limiting factor of external camouflage only, the barges and floating material around *Köln* do a nice job of breaking up the ship's outline and merging it with the shore. The work should have been continued amidships where the dark of water showing through tends to spoil the effect. Even at that, *Köln* was probably safe from being spotted by casual observation from an aircrew flying overhead. Hiding from aerial cameras was another matter. The greatest flaw in *Köln*'s positioning was the stringing of very obvious, and generally unnecessary, anti-torpedo nets.[18] Once a photo interpreter's eye was drawn to the area by the characteristic 'string of pearls' pattern of floats of the torpedo barrier, finding the cruiser was no trick at all.

A more detailed look at camouflage nets, floating constructions and camouflage material on a ship

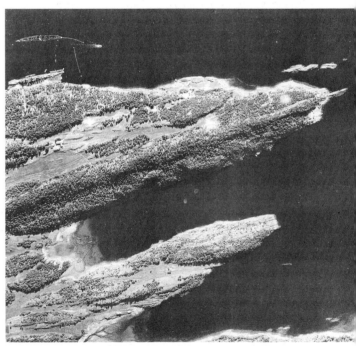

3-20 German light cruiser *Köln* hidden in Foetten Fjord, Norway, by floating material tying her outline into the shoreline, 19 July 1942.

superstructure is possible on photographs showing how all three were used to disguise the German battleship *Tirpitz* in Aasfjord in 1942 (photo 3-21). Nearly vertical fjord walls permitted the huge warship to snuggle within a few feet of the land. Nets were draped over the big guns and used to connect amidships to the shore. More nets and floating material were used to break up the characteristic shape of the hull and kill shadows. The good work was, as usual, obviated by the bad.

---

16. The photographer was standing on one side of the water space and buildings can be seen immediately behind the camouflaged ships.

17. Note that Köln's characteristic offset after turrets show clearly. The rearmost turret is right of the ship's centreline and its mate is offset to the left of (the bow of the ship is to the left).

---

18. The fjord was so steep and narrow that a broadside torpedo attack was impossible for lack of distance to let the torpedo stabilise its run depth. A stern-on attack might have been possible up the open reach of the fjord to the right, but the narrow angle involved would have necessitated an unusually accurate shot.

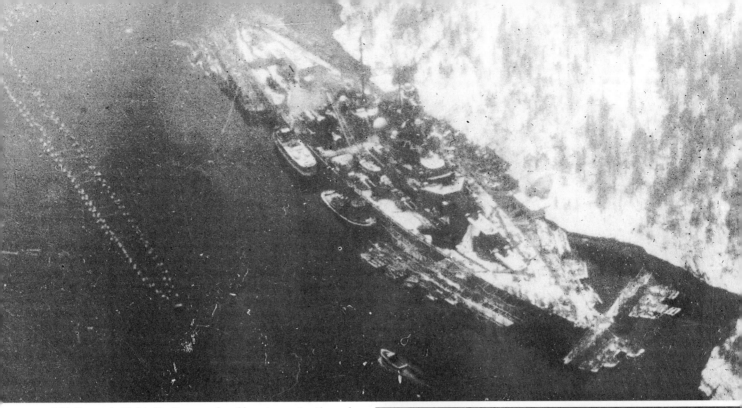

3-21 *German battleship* Tirpitz *camouflaged by nets, construction and floating material to break up her outline next to the shore. Aasfjord, Norway, 15 February 1942.*

3-22 *Enlargement of a camouflaged Japanese carrier showing nets and floating material. Note the shadow cast by the carrier's island.*

Additional floating material should have merged the bow and stern to the shore more completely. In another critical error the torpedo net floats show clearly. This camouflage also shows the problem of seasonal variations. Snow on the ship and shore should also have been carried through as a major theme on the netting. Indeed, snow did collect on the barges, adding to their effectiveness as camouflage. What snow had collected on the netting seems to be weighing it down.

Nets Plus

On the far side of the world at the end of the war sorties by the Japanese navy were rare, so ships could be completely covered with camouflage as protection from American bombers. The Japanese became adept at breaking up a ship outline (photo 3-22). Nets and floating material nicely disrupted the basic carrier shape and the netting effectively killed hull shadows. However, in this example a shadow from the ship's island shows clearly. Another flaw was the tented netting on the flight deck which had its highest points making a straight line down the centre of the ship.[19] When seen in its overall context the carrier camouflage in photo 3-22 is less impressive (photo 3-23). The two very obvious carriers call attention to their better disguised neighbour. Lest the photo interpreter's job seem too simple, the photography on which the

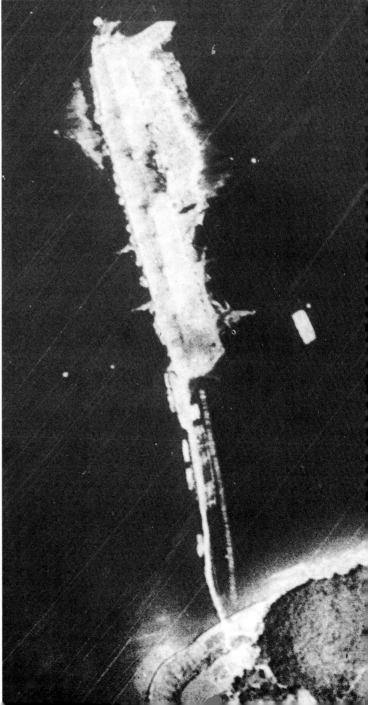

19. The World War II annotation identified this carrier as *Hayataka*. No such ship existed. It was probably either *Aso* or *Ikoma*, both uncompleted carriers that were seriously damaged by US naval aircraft from TF 38 three weeks after these photos were taken. The camouflage of these ships and others nearby, was good enough to protect them from a number of US Navy air strikes during which the hidden ships were not found.

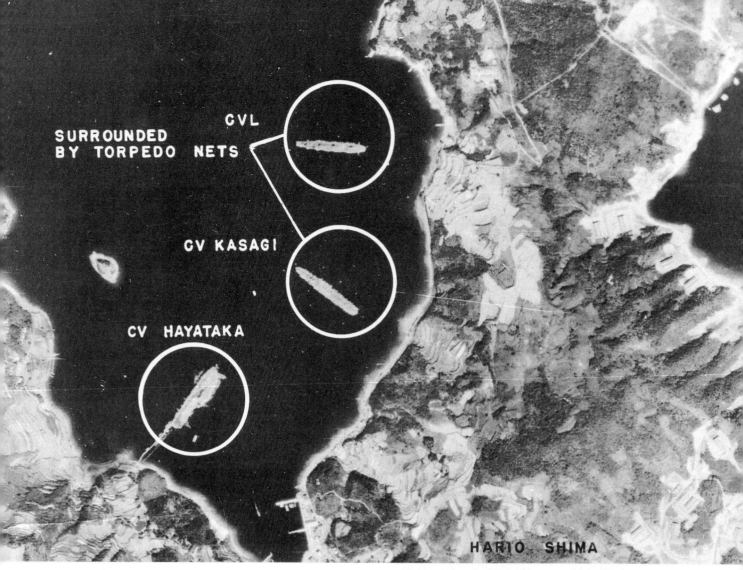

SURROUNDED
BY TORPEDO NETS

CVL

CV KASAGI

CV HAYATAKA

HARIO SHIMA

3-23 The carrier in photo 3-22 shown in its background context.

3-24 The Japanese carriers in photo 3-23 were found by a XXI Bomber Command photo interpreter near Sasebo, Japan, using small scale photography on 2 July 1945.

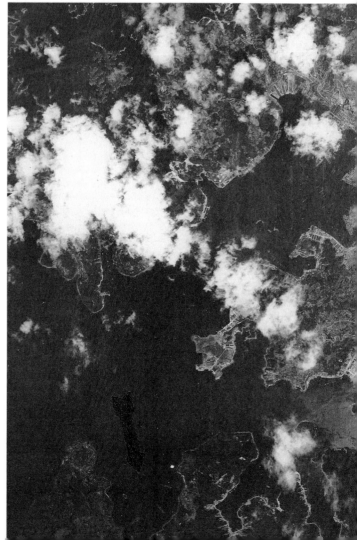

three Japanese carriers were first located is included for comparison (photo 3-24). This imagery was one of hundreds of small scale low-contrast photos taken by a single XXI Bomber Command F-13 (photoreconnaissance version of a B-29), flying at 28,000 feet (8,500 m). Every inch of every photo had to be scanned to find the faint shapes of Japanese carriers. These were hiding in a bay near Sasebo, Japan.[20]

Even better camouflage of a carrier occurred near Kure, Japan (photo 3-25). Tented nets broke up the flat expanse of the flight deck. Floating material and painted nets were expertly used to join the Japanese carrier *Ryuho* to the shore in a realistic manner. Had netting been used to kill the pronounced shadow from the carrier's hull, this camouflage might have been nearly perfect. In another example from the Kure area, two Japanese carriers were unusually well tied to their background context by nets and

20. Photo interpretation of Japanese targets was made more difficult because of a lack of cultural experience and comparative coverage such as PIs working in Europe enjoyed. Even a superficial check of a coastline using comparisons from earlier missions (had there been any) would have made detection of the carefully camouflaged Japanese ship a matter of child's play. As it was, PIs working Japan usually had to find well hidden targets in unfamiliar areas – often seen for the first time.

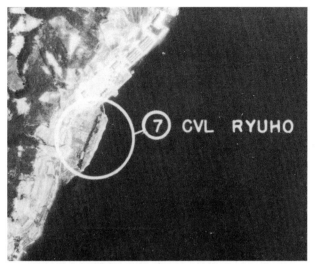

3-25 *The Japanese light carrier* Ryuho *was very well camouflaged near Kure, Japan, 28 May 1945. Its shadow gave it away.*

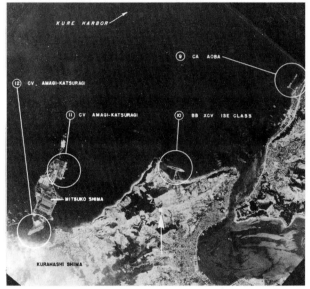

3-26 *A pair of Japanese Unryu class carriers exceptionally well blended into their environment with nets and floating material. Kure, Japan, 22 June 1945.*

3-27 *Enlargement of photo 3-26. The carriers' shapes were discernible, but only with time to study the scene.*

floating material (photo 3-26). Other warships in the area called a photo interpreter's attention to a more detailed search. Without comparative photo coverage the shape of the little island was unknown, thus extensions made by the camouflaged carriers had to be found the hard way. In an enlargement (photo 3-27) the island's real outline, as well as the basic shape of the carriers, can be discerned – but this camouflage work was very good. Only careful study and stereo viewing gave these ships away. Note the absence of revealing shadows. The use of nets to avoid shadows was excellent. The flaw was that the painted muslin nets were simply too thin and the camera looked right through them, giving the net camouflaged portions a filmy appearance not shared by the land and ships. A second layer of painted muslin a foot of so underneath would have been extremely effective.

At Yokosuka Naval Base (near Yokohama) in May 1945, the Japanese put together one of the best naval camouflage jobs I have seen (photo 3-28). The battleship *Nagato* was exceptionally well hidden, but not well enough to avoid damage from TF 38 aircraft on 18 July.[21] There were a number of old warships and a few small combatants in plain sight, but *Nagato* was almost perfectly disguised.[22] A few small shadows were about all that marred her painted net and floating construction camouflage. Try to find her.[23]

Ports

If it was almost impossible to camouflage a ship effectively, trying to camouflage a port was a real fool's errand. The basic problem was that ports were on pre-war maps and could usually be located easily – even at night – by nearby geographical or cultural features. The configuration of a coast, bends in rivers and converging patterns of land transportation could all be used to locate a port – and those 'pointers' were too big to camouflage.

The small oil port of Pangkalansoesoe on Sumatra, offers a good example of a fine camouflage/deception job. It also illustrates the inability of even very good camouflage to cover a port area when the overall geographic context cannot be altered. A pre-camouflage photo from August 1943 shows the key elements of the port: the government jetty and other piers and wharves

21. *Nagato* survived the war and the first Bikini Atoll A-bomb test, then sank during the second test in July 1946.

22. The old battleship at the upper left of photo 3-28 looks odd because it is up on the shore. *Mikasa* was Admiral Togo's flagship in the Battle of Tsu-Shima in 1905, where Japan defeated the Russian fleet. The battleship was set in concrete in the early 1920s to keep it from counting against Japan's tonnage quota following the 1922 Washington Naval Disarmament Treaties. I toured her in 1960 and as far as I know she is still there next to Yokosuka Navy Base.

23. *Nagato's* location is shown in Appendix II.

3-28 One of the best jobs of naval camouflage I have seen. Yokosuka, Japan, 31 May 1945. Can you find the hidden Japanese battleship Nagato? *(See Appendix II for the answer)*

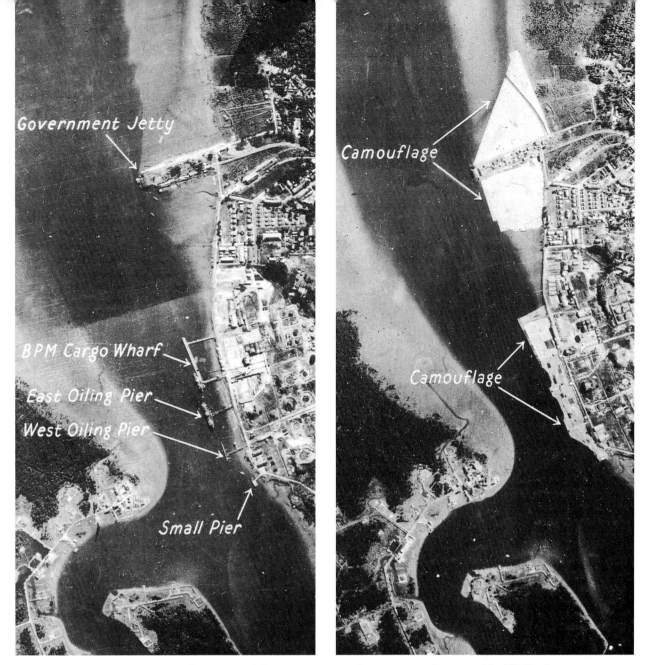

3-29 Before and after camouflage of a small oil port, Pangkalansoesoe, Sumatra. A decoy target was also presented for Allied bombers.

(photo 3-29). The right side of this photo pair, from January 1945, discloses extensive (if futile) camouflage work on the jetty, piers and wharf. A dummy pier was offered to Allied airmen, but it led nowhere and fooled no one. Obviously, having comparative photo cover from before the camouflage was added made the detection job much easier. The ease of finding this port, even at night, is illustrated by an oblique view (photo 3-30). If the convergence of land transport lines and the town itself were not unique enough in the middle of dense jungle, then the river pattern was distinctive enough to permit easy target identification. Three oil storage tanks going up in smoke offer proof that Allied airmen were not fooled.

Smoke

In Europe, where all the major port facilities were well known and aerial photo coverage was the rule rather than the exception, camouflage of a port was recognised as impossible. However, key aiming points might be obscured to confuse Allied bomb-aimers. The Germans rapidly expanded their use of smoke as Allied bomber raids grew in strength. A

200 per cent increase in smoke-defended targets was observed between October 1942 and June 1943.[24] In addition, the smoke density became heavier as new chemicals were used and the average number of generators jumped from 10 or 12 per site to over 350 at some targets.[25] About 15 minutes warning was all that was needed to get a good smoke defence built up.

Establishing a good smoke screen defence was directly dependent upon temperature, humidity, the nature of the surrounding terrain and wind. A wind too strong or in the wrong direction, would dissipate the smoke screen. Too weak a wind and the individual smoke generations would not join to form a smoke blanket.[26] Despite the unavoidable problems inherent in smoke screens they provided an excellent passive defence before the advent of radar bombing. As easily located coastal targets the

24. All confirmed by aerial photography.

25. The 'smoke' was actually sprayed droplets of chlorosulfonic acid, a harmless chemical that was easy to mass produce.

26. An ideal wind was between 10 and 12 miles per hour.

3-30 A wide area oblique shot shows why the Pangkalansoesoe camouflage was largely a waste of time. The town was too unique in its setting to hide.

German-controlled continental ports were naturally prime candidates for smoke defences.

Wilhelmshaven on the north-western German coast offers a good example of an obscuring smoke defence gone awry (photo 3-31). This photo shows American B-17s sliding overhead and bombs going off in the water and just short of the port.[27] It was poor bombing rather than the smoke that saved the port on 11 June 1943. Unfortunate winds and a late start[28] on the smoke screen resulted in the broad expanse of the Jade estuary being covered while the port itself was exposed. When warning and wind co-operated, a smoke defence could be very complete (photo 3-32). Brest, France, was often so blanketed that point target bombing was impossible and even area bombing was ineffective.[29]

German smoke generators came in all sizes from small one-time-use tubes to larger units that could

be resupplied with chemical fuel (photo 3-33). Many generators had to be started by hand, while others could be initiated remotely.[30] Permanent chemical generator sites were the most efficient, since they started fast, were reliable, and gave off a dense smoke that hung low to the ground (photo 3-34).

German smoke countermeasures were only used when necessary. A lone American F-5 (photo-reconnaissance version of the P-38) at high altitude was obviously a photoreconnaissance aircraft from England, and resulted in only a few generators being turned on at Kiel on 19 May 1943 (photo 3-35).[31] German Intelligence's use of aerial photos in bomb damage assessment work was primitive compared to Allied techniques, so the Luftwaffe did not fully appreciate that hiding a target from Allied

3-31 Even bombing of a distinctive port location like Wilhelmshaven, Germany, could be disrupted by smoke – but the wind had to co-operate. 11 June 1943.

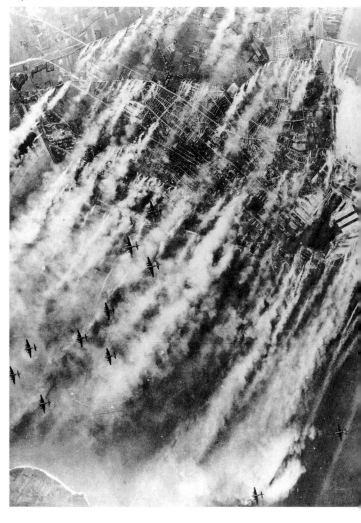

27. This raid on Wilhelmshaven's U-boat yards was made by 168 planes of VIII Bomber Command. In contemporary reports enemy fighters were given credit for precluding accurate bombing.

28. Apparently a diversionary strike on Cuxhaven, 30 miles to the north-east, achieved its purpose and Wilhelmshaven was caught off guard. Some of the smoke generators obviously have just been started.

29. Also note the black puffs of flak bursts. Two groups of US heavy bombers (77 planes) raided here and at Lorient. Fortunately their targets were the ports themselves – anywhere in the port would do.

30. Most generators had to be started by hand and were commonly spaced out along roads surrounding a target so crews could drive along pre-planned routes to touch them off from a motorcycle or vehicle.

31. The F-5 was collecting bomb-damage assessment photography after a raid by 102 heavy bombers earlier in the day.

3-32 Brest, France, under very effective smoke defences, 16 April 1943.

3-33 Three types of German chemical smoke generators. Two feature an umbrella-like diffuser to spread smoke faster.

3-34 A German smoke generator in operation. Chemical smoke was designed to stay near the surface so it did not dissipate rapidly.

intelligence was as important as covering it from bombers. Covering targets from bombers they certainly did – with characteristic thoroughness.[32] Kiel had been solidly under a smoke blanket when B-17s arrived earlier in the daytime on 19 May (photo 3-36).

The naval base and port areas of Kiel were thoroughly bombed on 25 July 1943 despite its formidable smoke screen.[33] Shifting winds were responsible for exposing parts of the port (photo 3-37). Note that smoke from generators (low to the ground) was blowing from lower left to upper right. Conversely, smoke from fires caused by the bombing (rising to higher altitudes) was blowing towards the upper left. Both smoke layers could have made things more difficult for subsequent bombardiers, but different winds at different altitudes served to prevent build-up of a generator and fire smoke blanket.

Allied intelligence carefully plotted the location of German smoke generators at Kiel (photo 3-38) in hopes that a clear edge on any side might give aircrews a better idea where the target lay. The plots show how the 360-degree nature of a good smoke defence was designed to gain some independence from the wind. Doubtless there were other smoke generators that were not in operation on the days in question because of their poor position relative to

32. Sometimes decoy smoke screens were used to get Allied bombers to drop ordnance harmlessly. The Kiel decoy screen was a few miles north-west at Eckernforde.

33. The 8th Air Force sent 218 heavy bombers to Hamburg and Kiel this day. Kiel was actually a side-show. On the night of 24/25 July more than 700 RAF heavies hit Hamburg. The RAF hit again for the next three nights and the US 8th during the day. By 27 July, Hamburg was engulfed in a fire storm that destroyed a large part of the city.

3-35 Kiel Harbour, 19 May 1943. Only a few smoke generators would be turned on for a lone high-flying reconnaissance plane.

the target and prevailing winds. When smoke worked it was impressive. Only a small patch of water showed at Kiel on 5 January 1944 (photo 3-39). Allied bombers had to dump ordnance into the general area of their targets because precision bombing was impossible.[34]

Radar

Later years of the war saw Allied bombers using the H2X navigation radar[35] to permit better target attack in spite of night, bad weather or smoke. Early scope photos show that US aircrews had a tool that was crude, but good enough to give a recognisable picture of large areas of the ground. Though not a detailed or delicate discriminator of the earth's physical features, the radar sets were good at showing land-water contrast (photo 3-40).

The presentation of such a radar showed a map-like view of the ground with the plane carrying the radar located at the centre of the scope. In this case the aircraft was near the southern coast of the Zuider Zee (the white spot just to the left of the

3-36 An oblique view of the Kiel smoke screen from 26,000 feet, taken during a bombing raid on 19 May 1943.

plane's position is Amsterdam). Of course, like any weapon of war, a counter was quickly sought to negate radar navigation. Radars could be jammed[36] but jamming techniques were so primitive they had little effect, so other defensive means were tried.

One of the most interesting and imaginative radar defeating systems was German research into

---

34. Over 200 heavy bombers from 8th Air Force hit Kiel on 5 January 1944.

35. American heavy bombers used H2X radar, the US version of Britain's H2S radar. The RAF first used radar for pathfinder target marking in January 1943, Eighth Air Force bombers got the system in September 1943 and Fifteenth Air Force in April 1944. In the Eighth Air Force, these navigation devices were supplemented by 'blind bombing' equipment in January 1944 (Gee-H) and August 1944 (Micro-H).

3-37 German smoke defences were regularly used against bombers – but even with widely dispersed generators, the wind had to co-operate. Kiel, 25 July 1943. Bombs are going off near the naval basin.

3-38 An intelligence report plotting smoke screens experienced at Kiel during the raid of photo 3-37.

the use of floating 'corner reflectors'[37] to spoof Allied airborne navigation radars with additional ground clutter (photo 3-41). Large numbers of the floating 'corner reflectors' could be moored to completely alter the presentation of land-water contrast on Allied radar sets (photo 3-42). Another use of these reflectors would be to simulate the radar return of a factory or city in hopes of causing bombs to be dropped harmlessly in a nearby lake. Useless under conditions of clear visibility, these simple, passive devices would have been quite effective at night or in bad weather to make a lake or characteristic landfall disappear for Allied navigators. They might have been equally effective in presenting bogus landfalls or targets. Being readily relocatable the floating reflectors could be re-arranged to appear differently in the day or night, or widely dispersed during the day to protect the deception.

A combination of widespread jamming and devices such as the reflectors used in large numbers

might have impeded the Allied bombing campaign. If deployed in large numbers and moved about the reflectors could have caused a lot of Allied bombs to go astray. Apparently the Germans either hit on the technique too late in the war, did not have the resources to implement it on a large scale, or did not realise how effective it might be. In any case, this passive electronic counter-measure had no impact on the war, nor could it have been anything but temporarily effective once Allied airmen controlled the skies over Germany and could come and go at will.[38] Besides, over time Allied photo intelligence would have spotted and plotted the reflectors' locations to permit bomber crews to make allowances for the 'incorrect' radar returns.

---

36. The strong strobe lines to the lower right are radio interference of some sort, possibly jamming from a distance in that direction.

37. A corner reflector bounces radar energy back to an emitter at a strength out of proportion to the size of the reflector, making it appear like a return from a much larger object.

38. The photos of corner reflectors included in this chapter are from a German report, dated 1944, that was picked up by US Intelligence at the end of the war. I can find no record of an Allied awareness of German experimental development of radar reflectors. If this is true, Germany could have achieved technical surprise over the Allies with large-scale deployment of these devices. The disruption of Allied radar-assisted bombing would have been effective until the spoof was discovered and countering procedures devised for aircrews – a matter of weeks at most.

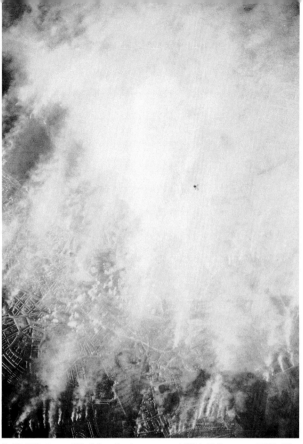

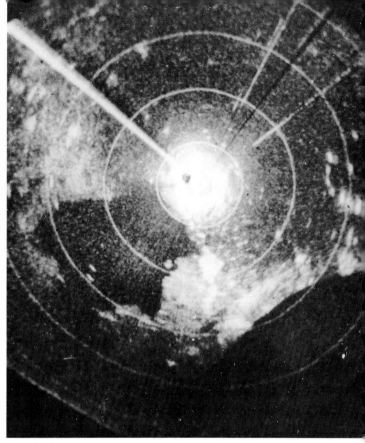

3-39 *What an Allied bomb aimer saw at Kiel, 5 January 1944. The single black puff was flak.*

3-40 *Smoke screens were useless against radar. Early US scope photo showing the Dutch coast and the south end of the Zuider Zee. The radar was an H2X in an Eighth Air Force B-17 of 482nd Bomber Group, 23 May 1944.*

3-41 (Inset) *One German attempt at a countermeasure to foil Allied airborne navigation radar: floating 'corner reflectors,' 1945.*

3-42 *Large numbers of corner reflectors used experimentally to change the shape of a shoreline presented to airborne radars. This electronic camouflage had the potential of denying Allied bombers recognition of key navigation points.*

CHAPTER 4

EAGLES AS SITTING DUCKS

Aircraft and Airfields

The great attacker in World War II, the most feared and most effective weapons system, was the aeroplane. It was also the primary defender since the natural enemy of an aeroplane is another aeroplane. In Europe, the German war machine ran through Poland, Denmark and Norway, the Low Countries, and France along paths made clear from the skies. British pursuit planes stopped the German advance westward during the Battle of Britain. When Hitler turned his attention to the Soviet Union, again his warbirds led the way. The RAF (later joined by American bombers) carried the war to Nazi Europe from the onset of conflict. The Allies' return to Europe and their subsequent advances were spearheaded from the air.

The same air orientation of the war was true in Asia. As American and British forces lost their air power in the Japanese advances of 1941 and early 1942, they were progressively less able to resist despite sometimes having superior numbers on the ground. Air power also led the Allies back through the Japanese Empire. Control of the air made new conquests possible which, in turn, permitted new airfields to be built closer to Japan. The new airfields resulted in Allied control of the air being extended and the cycle repeated. The aeroplane was also Japan's final defence, and bombing of the Japanese home islands resulted in eventual surrender.

Small wonder that considerable camouflage attention was given to air-related offensive and defensive capability. Aircraft are relatively difficult to destroy while flying but are terribly vulnerable on the ground. Unlike tanks, artillery pieces or ships, planes are thin-skinned and easily destroyed even by small calibre weapons. Near miss explosions could easily make delicate aircraft non-operational even if they were not destroyed.

Airfields and landing grounds were equally vulnerable. The broad grass fields or wide paved runways had to be open and level. In normal use they were designed to be readily identified from the air by pilots. This (as one would expect) also made them easy for intelligence analysts to locate on aerial photography. The huge hangars necessary for aircraft repair stood out from their surroundings and were easy to destroy. Even temporary tactical airfields with modest aircraft servicing facilities were generally simple to detect, hard to defend, and easy pickings for raiding planes. Loss of planes on the ground, available landing strips and minimal

service capacity seriously limited the ability of an air unit to perform its mission. Passive defence of air assets therefore played a large role in 'evening up the odds' for a defender. The further one side or the other was driven onto the defensive, the more important camouflage became to them.

Painting Planes

Aircraft camouflage presented the camoufleur with an interesting problem. With a few notable exceptions, a paint scheme optimised to reduce visibility in the air would make the plane very conspicuous on the ground.[1] Conversely, painted patterns and colours aimed at blending with trees, brush, or shadows would stand out starkly against a pale sky. For this reason, nearly all World War II aircraft camouflage schemes featured two distinct paint patterns: one designed against view from above and the side, the other for camouflage to minimise detection or identification from below.

Day flyers commonly got a light blue or grey paint job for the undersides of wings, tail, and fuselage. This made the aircraft blend into the sky when viewed from below and worked against other aircraft as well as observation from the ground (photos 4-1 and 4-2). Night flyers were painted matt black on their undersurfaces. The lower their normal attack altitude, the higher on the fuselage the black extended (photo 4-3). When RAF home fields were no longer in jeopardy, many of their night raiding aircraft were painted aeroplane black all over.[2]

High altitude photoreconnaissance aircraft were an interesting exception to the 'light belly' rule. At high altitude the sky progressively darkens and a light underside would have made them stand out.[3] Aircraft that routinely operated above 30,000 feet were often given a dark-coloured aeroplane paint scheme – something short of black but decidedly on

---

1. Camouflage was never used as decoration or a cover coat for an aeroplane. The paint added weight, sometimes hundreds of pounds, thus degraded the performance of the aircraft. Aircraft camouflage was a matter of improving survival.

2. Aircraft with a night attack mission were painted black to help avoid searchlights. Before the advent of radar-equipped night-fighters and anti-aircraft guns, searchlights were the greatest threat to a night raider. If a bomber was caught in the cone of two or more lights, guns on the ground and enemy fighter planes could attack.

3. At higher altitudes there are fewer particles of dust or water vapour to reflect sunlight. At very high altitudes the sky is black.

4-1 German Ju 88 in 1940 showing an abrupt transition from the light toned 'sky-blend' on undersurfaces to the darker 'ground blend' on the top.

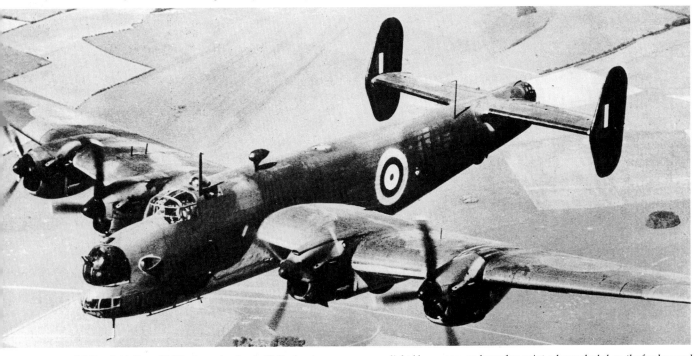

4-2 Royal Air Force Halifax heavy bomber in 1942, showing a very narrow light blue or grey undersurface paint scheme shaded up the fuselage and engine nacelles.

the dark side. For RAF and US reconnaissance planes this colour was a dull medium-dark blue with just a touch of grey mixed in. Since it was used almost exclusively for photoreconnaissance planes this shade was dubbed 'PR blue' (photo 4-4).

Aircraft upper surface paint jobs were as varied as the backgrounds they sought to blend with and the imaginations of their painters. Desert aircraft got pale shades of tan, yellow or grey which were often mottled with black, brown or dark grey. Naval aircraft usually stuck to single-colour paint schemes on upper surfaces.[4] This was normally done in a shade of dark blue-grey to blend with the water background, protecting aircraft flying low and viewed from above (photo 4-5). In winter, aircraft might get white upper surfaces where snow cover was extensive and enemy attack a danger. Where snow was less common, winter camouflage colours tended towards dark browns and greens. For land

aircraft in the spring, summer and fall, lighter, and brighter, browns and greens were mixed with occasional yellows or black in a bewildering number of combinations and patterns.[5]

The most common paint patterns for aircraft camouflage were random and mottle.[6] In the random pattern, irregular bands of alternating colours were designed to disrupt the straight lines of the plane, thereby making it harder to see (photo 4-6). In the case of low flyers, such as the Fairey Battle light bomber, camouflage of this type also afforded some protection while airborne (photo 4-7). Enemy fighter pilots at higher altitudes might not see the low flying camouflaged plane against the background of the earth unless its movement caught their eye. The example Battle even had its glass canopy painted over, trading crew visibility for some invisibility from overhead.

---

4. British naval aircraft were sometimes painted in a landplane-style random disruption pattern of two colours. This camouflage could be a dark blue-grey and a lighter grey or dark blue-grey and dark grey-green. The latter combination was fondly referred to as 'slime and sewage'.

5. Other colours used occasionally were rust, pink, violet, purple, maroon, white and dark blue.

6. Both of these broadly used patterns had as many 'official' and unofficial names as there were variations on the two themes. The terms random and mottle are the most descriptive to me.

Dozens of books have been written on aircraft camouflage used in different theatres at different times by the various warring nations. The number of different combinations was incredible, particularly early in the war. In many cases, before these days of computer-determined optimum camouflage patterns, each individual plane had a unique application of a few standard colours (photo 4-8). Typical colour combinations were brown and tan, brown and green, and three-colour combinations such as olive drab, brown and grey.[7] Mottled patterns were usually dark flecks or

splotches of colour on a lighter background, designed to blend the plane into shadows on the ground (photos 4-9 to 4-11). Spray painting, when available, made possible the subtleties of colour transition necessary for really effective mottle patterns.

By mid-1943 pattern camouflage for American army aircraft gave way to mono-chromatic paint jobs using either olive drab or medium-to-light brown (photo 4-12).[8] By the spring of 1944 unpainted aircraft were becoming common, starting with fighters. Later that year unpainted American

---

7. There were 'official' names to precisely identify very specific shades of each colour. Some of the names were Ocean Grey, Medium Sea Grey, Neutral Grey, Sand, Dark Earth, Earth Brown, Flight Blue, Medium Green, Dark Green, and various shades of Olive Drab. Many of these shades also had unofficial names given by the troops. Desert Pink became 'tittie pink', and one can easily guess the local terminology for Medium Brown.

8. As early as October 1943 the decision to camouflage US Army aircraft was delegated to local commanders in the field and aircraft production facilities no longer applied a coat of olive drab as part of the delivery contract.

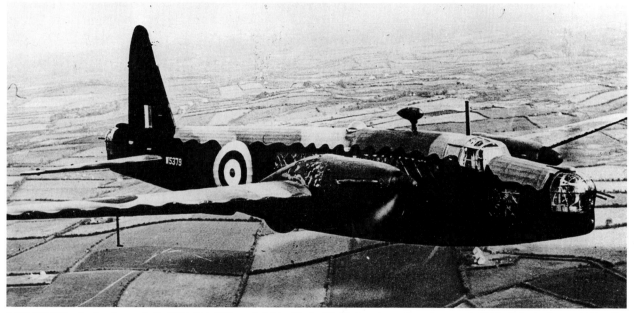

4-3 RAF Wellington bomber, probably 1943. This 'Wimpey' night raider had its black undersurface paint extended high on the fuselage and only token camouflage to protect it on the ground in daylight.

4-4 Unarmed RAF photoreconnaissance Spitfire XI painted in 'PR blue' to blend with the dark sky at high altitude. (Smithsonian)

4-5 US Navy F-4Fs at Efate, New Hebrides, 10 September 1942. These planes were painted a sea-blending matt medium grey-blue on top and grey-white underneath to blend with the sky when viewed from below.

4-6 RAF Battle light bomber painted with a common brown and tan random camouflage pattern. (Smithsonian)

4-7 US Army P-40s in a camouflage test involving various combinations of tan, brown and green. Bolling Field, Washington DC, 18 October 1942.

4-8 US Navy PBYs at Olongapo, Philippines, 26 May 1941. The colour combinations were identical but no two planes were painted with the same placement of shape-disrupting alternating bands, showing the 'home grown' origin of the camouflage.

4-9 Italian Cant Z.1007bis, probably in 1941. The plane had a sand-coloured base mottled with black or dark brown to blend into desert shadows.

4-10 German Hs 129 in North Africa in 1942. The light grey with occasional small black mottles blended well with a stark landscape dominated by small random shadows. (Smithsonian)

4-11 Japanese Ki-61 'Tony' (with propeller spinner removed) at Boram Airfield, New Guinea, 16 October 1943. A base of light grey was overlaid with a dark green mottle pattern to blend with jungle foliage.

4-12 B-25s medium bombers of the US 12th Bomber Group in Egypt, 1942. The standard olive drab plane stood out while Desert Sand paint jobs on the others made them blend into the background.

planes, including bombers, were more often the rule than the exception (photo 4-13).[9] Bare metal combat planes were a sure signal that the home fields of the aircraft were not in danger of air attack and there was nothing to be gained from camouflage. The only other warring power to routinely use unpainted aircraft was Japan.

Decoy Planes

Aircraft decoys served several basic purposes. They were supposed to make the enemy believe that a dormant airfield was active, that an active field had greater strength, or to enhance the credibility of a dummy airfield. Another major function of decoy aircraft was to provide attackers additional targets to pull weapons away from real planes. A good decoy had to be more obvious than the planes it served to protect – but not too obvious. A decoy also had to look enough like a real plane to convince an attacker for the few seconds necessary to upset his aim or draw his ordnance. Only a rare few decoys were ever good enough to fool photo interpreters.

The most basic decoy was a painted or cut-out silhouette. Silhouette decoys were marginally effective at night if properly lit by simulated fires from bomb damage or hangar lights. They were of little value in daylight. Painted silhouettes cast no shadows and had to be maintained or parts of the shape would fade away (photo 4-14).[10] Cut-out silhouettes were more believable if raised off the ground the height and angle of a landing gear so

9. These 12th Bomb Group planes were anything but uniform. All carried British style tail-fin flashes and the US national insignia were standardised, but some aircraft carried it on both wings and others just on the upper left and lower right. In addition, two of the B-25s bore a vertical stripe on the leading edge of their vertical stabilisers.

10. Note that some of the planes painted on the dark splotches have parts of their outline fading away, or not yet painted. Some of the aircraft in the neighbouring field may be the same type of painted decoy with the work completed by toning down the paving material used as a background. I think these are all decoys but without stereo viewing and coverage at several different times it is difficult to tell.

4-13 Eighth Air Force B-17s of the 92nd Bomber Group on their way to Ruhland, Germany, 28 May 1944. An older plane was painted olive drab, but a replacement aircraft showed bare metal – a sure sign that the home field was no longer in danger of attack.

they cast good wing shadows. However, cut-outs did not have believable shadows from the fuselage and vertical stabiliser (photo 4-15). Naturally they also had a flat look that might not be apparent to the naked eye but was always very apparent to stereo-viewing on intelligence photography.

The next step up in decoy reality was a crude construction that was fully three-dimensional. If a crude decoy would not stand up to direct observation, it could be enhanced by a masking drape of camouflage netting (photo 4-16). Carefully designed light, simple decoys, made of canvas over a wood framework, could be very credible when viewed from beyond a quarter of a mile away (photo 4-17).[11] Lightweight inflatable rubber decoys were even better because they had good three-dimensional shapes and could be painted with

---

11. This ultra-lightweight RAF decoy was held down by two bands tied to what were probably sand-filled ammunition boxes.

4-14 German photo of RAF Tern Hill (roughly 30 miles NW of Birmingham), 27 September 1940. Decoy bombers were painted on a thin coat of paving material. The Germans photographed the work before it was completed.

4-15 Simple cut-out aircraft decoys being tested at Mitchell Field, New York, 23 February 1943. These decoys cast a partially credible shadow, but they were obviously flat and unreal.

realistic detail.[12] Some inflated decoys were so well done that they stood up to viewing from only a few dozen yards away (photo 4-18).

The problem with inflated decoys was that they needed constant attention (photo 4-19). If a single decoy was detected it called all the others into more careful scrutiny and few decoys could withstand a really good look. The few that could were elaborate three-dimensional constructions showing a lot of detail. The British made some of the best (photo 2-20).

The example was a Brewster Buffalo decoy that had a proper propeller, good looking landing gear, realistically shaped wings, a Pitot tube on the right wing, and radio antenna. This decoy also had an authentic paint job and markings. Lack of a motor and cockpit glass were cleverly masked by canvas covers of a type routinely used on real aircraft.

When viewed from the perspective of an attacker, the British Brewster Buffalo decoy had few flaws (photo 4-21). Compared with a real Buffalo, the decoy fuselage showed the lines of its framework, and the near wing was warped. Otherwise, this decoy was excellent. The other decoy in the example photo, a Blenheim bomber, was also very well done. Its only flaws were the braces necessary to hold up the flimsy wings.

The final category of decoy was the use of non-operational aircraft. Real aircraft as decoys had the advantage of extreme authenticity, if they were not too badly damaged (photo 4-22). If the decoys were missing key parts, or so badly beat up that they no longer looked like active aircraft, they ceased to have value as decoys (photo 4-23). Mixing operational aircraft in with decoys gave attackers a 'target-rich environment' – more targets than they could cope with – thus saving some of the real planes from destruction (photo 4-24).[13] The Japanese made extensive and effective use of non-flyable planes positioned with operational aircraft.

For the photo interpreter, one of the most telling signatures of a decoy was lack of movement. If comparative coverage of a field showed the same plane in exactly the same place, no matter how good the decoy construction, a PI would not be fooled. Other signatures for identifying decoys or finding actual aircraft were oil stains, tracks on unimproved surfaces and areas of grass blown to dirt where engines were run up.

Hiding Planes

An aircraft on the ground was not only a 'sitting duck', it was usually very easy to see from the air. Thus, the first line of aircraft passive defence was its own camouflage, but that alone was not enough. Enemy day-bombers and certainly enemy

---

12. Inflatable rubber dummies worked best for aircraft since the planes had smooth rounded shapes. Other military equipment tended to be more angular with protrusions that did not lend themselves to reproduction in rubber. The smooth rubber shapes of aircraft decoys could also be easily painted to better represent an aeroplane.

---

13. On 3 April 1944, more than 300 US B-24s, B-25s, A-20s, and P-38s ravaged Hollandia destroying or damaging most of the Japanese planes in the area.

4-16 A crude Japanese decoy aeroplane was given a drape of camouflage netting to add to its authenticity.

4-17 British decoy aircraft in Libya. The nicely rounded construction cast a realistic shadow and would have stood up to all but short-range observation.

4-18 Double deception at Dinjan Airfield in India. A fake native house with bamboo mat shades hid a fighter plane revetment. The plane was a very realistic inflated rubber P-40 decoy.

4-19 Decoys needed attention to remain credible. Dinjan, India, 1943.

4-20 A remarkably detailed wooden decoy of an RAF Brewster Buffalo fighter. England, 31 July 1941.

4-21 The Brewster Buffalo decoy parked with a real Buffalo and a decoy Blenheim. England, 31 July 1941.

4-22 *The best decoy aircraft was a real plane that was no longer flyable – but it could not be too badly wrecked. Boram Airfield in Japanese held New Guinea, 16 October 1943.*

4-23 *Two former Armée de l'Air Bloch MB.152c pursuit planes (sans engines and wheels) used as decoys by the Germans at St. Rambert airfield, France (south of Lyon), 20 February 1945. The mottle camouflage paintwork appears to have been two shades of grey and two of green.*

4-24 *Derelict Japanese aircraft parked with operational aircraft gave US raiders a target selection problem. Hollandia, New Guinea, 3 April 1944. Only five planes on the near taxi-way were 'live' aircraft.*

4-25 German Bf 109 fighter in France in 1940 hidden in a rough sand-bagged revetment along a tree line with freshly cut branches draped for good measure. The plane was camouflaged with an overall light grey with a dark slate-grey spine.

4-26 Bamboo stalks cut away and side shoots bent over formed a natural hangar. A few cut stalks served for a door; Dinjan, India, 1942.

intelligence collectors had no difficulty finding planes parked in the open protected only by paint.

The easiest and fastest way to hide a plane on the ground was to back it into a line of trees or bushes and cover it with natural vegetation (photo 4-25). This technique worked best when combined with a complementary camouflage paint job. The amount of cut vegetation used to hide an aeroplane was in direct proportion to the ground crew's perception of the degree of danger tempered by the requirement to get the aircraft airborne (photo 4-26). Having to remove an excessive amount of natural material before the plane could be used obviously got in the way of operations.

Even out in the open, a suitably painted aircraft might be credibly camouflaged with the addition of a few cut branches (photo 4-27). Of course, this type of cover did not stand up to review by a photo interpreter, but it might afford some protection against a fast, low-flying raider (photo 4-28). Enough natural material and proper positioning allowed even a twin-engined bomber to virtually disappear. However, it was possible to overdo a good thing. Excessive piling of cut branches attracted attention and made it difficult to get the plane into action (photo 4-29). 'Brush piles' hiding planes also made it almost impossible to perform maintenance on the aircraft.

An alternative to good paint and natural camouflage for aircraft was simply to cover them from observation. Enemy planes might guess that a target lurked under the covering, but its identification was made difficult or impossible. In a sense, cover camouflage was more directed against enemy intelligence than against attackers. So much the better if the cover also made the target harder to hit.

A crude but effective cover camouflage was provided by the Japanese when they draped parked aircraft with wide mats of woven palm fronds (photo 4-30). Where natural material was less abundant or less appropriate, drapes of a variety of net, mesh, or cloth served the same purpose. Painted canvas was a popular base for aircraft cover camouflage (photo 4-31).[14] The next best cover, and the most widely used, was netting (photo 4-32).[15]

Aircraft Netting

Camouflage netting for aircraft came in a considerable variety of styles, widths, and patterns – with a corresponding spectrum of effectiveness. Since netting was generally transparent to enemy intelligence photography, the camouflage nets were primarily designed to make aiming harder for an attacking plane (photo 4-33). To be really effective, netting had to be simple to set up, easy to get the plane into and out of, and capable of breaking up the straight lines and shadows of the aircraft. The main types of netting were: plain, painted, garnished, and strip.

Plain or painted mesh nets were of negligible utility except to kill shadows (photo 4-34). They were light and easy to get off the plane for a fast take-off so they continued in use long after the general recognition that they hid little. The most common technique was to suspend the netting on corner poles so that it covered an aircraft parked in the open or an aircraft revetment. Strip netting was a way to use light net or mesh and still get a dense camouflage pattern. This type of netting was made by sewing short strips of coloured cloth onto a fishnet base. The cloth pieces could be in either a regular or irregular pattern. A variation was to use bands of fishnet to hold together long strips of coloured cloth. Strip netting was excellent for disrupting the lines of a plane and its shadow. If the pattern was compatible with the background, strip netting could be very effective.

Strip nets were in use before World War II began and some of the first put to the test were in Poland in 1939 (photo 4-35). However, since this elaborate

---

14. Canvas covered more completely than netting and denied all visual observation. Canvas could also be painted to blend into almost any background, but it was heavy, awkward to handle and a nightmare to maintain against a load of snow or heavy rain.

15. Aircraft netting was easily produced, transported, and handled. It was light and flexible and could be garnished with available materials to increase camouflage effectiveness.

4-27 Japanese aircraft painted to blend with jungle foliage. A few fresh fronds made a temporary disguise. Alexishafen, New Guinea, 9 November 1943.

4-28 Well done natural camouflage could even stand up in the open. Can you find the Japanese bomber? Cape Gloucester, Bismarcks (New Britain Is.), 21 May 1943. (See Appendix II for solution.)

4-29 Natural camouflage could be carried too far. These 'brush piles' on a Japanese airfield only tended to attract attention. New Guinea, 1943.

4-30 Woven palm frond matting completely covering a Japanese fighter on Tarawa, December 1943.

4-31 Painted camouflage material covering a parked aircraft or dispersal point, England, 1940.

4-32 Camouflage netting that appeared opaque or semi-opaque to the naked eye was transparent before the aerial camera. British photo of German netting covering temporary hangars at an airfield in France, 4 July 1942.

netting was employed on a well known airfield its effectiveness was diminished.

The Japanese were heavy users of strip nets, combining fishnet with coloured silk. This netting was most effective when it spread well beyond the aircraft it hid (photo 4-36). The example, from Hollandia, New Guinea, was selected to show the design and construction of the net; it was not a good use of the net. In this case the colour and tone of the netting was a contrast, not a blend, with the background. In addition, the wing line of the plane showed clearly. The same style of Japanese strip netting was used more effectively at an airfield near Rabaul in 1943 (photo 4-37).[16] Rather than draped, the nets were strung over revetments to screen their contents. Certainly there was no hope of hiding the fact that there were aircraft on a well established field. This netting denied intelligence and could distract a raider. These strip nets also appear to have been painted in addition to their basic colour patterns.

Garnish netting was mesh or fishnet with small pieces or tufts of cloth or natural material added to create random patterns. Light weight garnish nets

cut shadows but were essentially transparent (photo 4-38). Heavily garnished nets could make an aircraft disappear but were not easy to use. A well done drape of thickly garnished netting would blend a plane into a convenient tree line (photo 4-39). Such a camouflage was a good defence against strafers because it easily blended into the surroundings. Well done camouflage using heavily garnished nets could even let a plane survive in the open if the site was carefully chosen (photo 4-40).

Garnish type netting found favour when land was changing hands rapidly and planes were operating out of temporary tactical fields. One disadvantage was the time it took to get a heavy net off an aircraft, thus making fast take-offs impossible. It was seldom worth the bother to use heavily garnished nets at a fixed, known, airfield location. It was easier to camouflage the shelters where the planes were parked, then simply put the planes inside.

Aircraft Parking

Disguising aircraft revetments and hangars was elevated to an artform in the years just prior to WW II. Some of the work was exceptional for imaginative design as well as for enthusiastic and detailed execution. Given enough time and effort, a few planes could be flawlessly hidden from view, albeit not necessarily in an operationally viable status.

A pre-war example serves to illustrate the point. At least five P-26s of the 3rd Pursuit Squadron were effectively hidden at Batangas, Philippines, during a camouflage exercise (photo 4-41). A small portion of one P-26 tail showed in an oblique view, but other net-draped pursuit planes were invisible (photo 4-42). But this camouflage occurred during a carefully prepared test. The planes were few in number, and not being actively used. It was a very different problem to hide large numbers of aircraft so they were both operationally viable and protected.

Dispersed parking was part of the answer to passively protecting aircraft (photo 4-43). Planes could be placed some distance apart in open fields, along existing road patterns or in forest patches (photos 4-44 and 4-45). Parking revetments and taxiways were obvious keys to the dispersal unless they too were camouflaged. It might be difficult to attack a squadron so spread out, but it was usually not hard to find them.

Early in the war the Luftwaffe began to embed aircraft parking revetments in urban settings in occupied countries (photo 4-46). This had the dual advantage of partially disguising the parking pattern and deterring an attack. If it were not for the prominent taxiways, British Intelligence might have taken the house-like aircraft shelters in the example photograph for part of the town.

Fake house shelters for aircraft were used by all the warring powers in a number of locations and

---

16. The US B-25 overhead was from the 38th Bomber Squadron, taking part in a 350-plane assault on Rabaul and its two airfields. This was the start of a major air offensive to isolate Rabaul in preparation for the invasion of Bougainville on 1 November 1943.

4-33 Nets covering revetments at a German airfield did not stop British Intelligence from identifying and counting the He 219 night-fighters underneath, 20 June 1943. Also note planes parked among the trees.

4-34 Escape from camouflage was important for a fast take-off. This 16 May 1941 British photo of one of their own airfields in Egypt was captioned 'Quick-release net for aircraft'.

for a wide variety of aircraft. Some of these camouflage attempts were pretty good (photo 4-47). When camouflage attention was also given to the taxiways this type of parking/shelter could easily escape casual detection. It would certainly have been difficult for a bomber at high altitude or at night, to spot some of the examples in these photos.

Hangars

The closer dispersed aircraft parking was to an airfield, the harder it was to hide. Aircraft parking around the perimeter of a landing area was expected and sought out by both attacking airmen

and intelligence technicians screening surveillance photography. To avoid becoming targets, even blast-proof hangars had to be disguised, or at least made harder to see (photo 4-48). Two favourite camouflage techniques for small hangars were the use of disruptive paint patterns and positioning the hangars in tree lines.

Hangars on an airfield proper were the hardest to disguise. Facilities at major fields, such as hangars, were usually large, obvious and commonly well

17. The hangars showing bare stringers through their roofs were damaged by an earlier German air raid during the invasion of France.

4-35 German photo of Polish strip netting, Rakow Airfield near Warsaw, 1939. The aircraft is a Bf 110.

4-36 Multi-coloured strip netting draped over a Japanese fighter and spread to the surrounding area to improve the blend with the ground. Hollandia, New Guinea, 3 April 1944.

4-37 Strip-netting augmented with a random two-colour pattern covered Japanese fighter revetments at Vaunakanau, Bismarcks, 12 October 1943.

4-38 Random garnished netting covering a parked B-23 as part of a 'Heavy Bomber Camouflage Net Test', Bolling Field, Washington DC, February 1942.

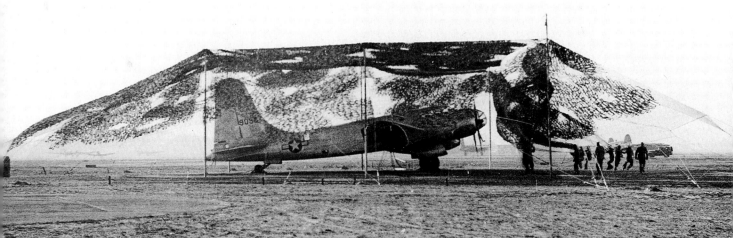

4-39 Heavily garnished netting and a convenient tree line were good camouflage if you did not have to move the plane in a hurry. The plane is a German Ju 87, France in 1940.

4-40 A Japanese fighter hiding in the open under a heavily garnished net during the US invasion of Zamboanga, Philippines, 10 March 1945. Smoke in the background was from naval onshore bombardment.

4-41 (Below) Vertical photo of a 3rd Pursuit Squadron field near Batangas, Philippines, 8 October 1940. In this camouflage test the field could be discerned but the planes were well hidden.

4-42 Oblique aerial photo of the 3rd Pursuit field at Batangas, Philippines, 8 October 1940. The tail of a P-26 pursuit ship can be seen in the fake hut where the aircraft was hidden. Locations where I think I see other planes are indicated by arrows. This is awfully good camouflage, but unlikely to work in a real operational environment.

4-43 German dispersed aircraft parking in open fields in Italy, RAF photo 25 June 1944. The taxiway gave the parking revetments away.

known to enemy intelligence from pre-war information. In the case of large permanent facilities, the best that could be hoped for was to make aim more difficult for a raiding bomber. At a field like Le Bourget, outside Paris, the painted camouflage toned down hangar roofs but did little to hide the structures (photo 4-49). Failure of the French to tone down the stark concrete of the parking apron undermined any marginal effectiveness of the hangar paint work.[17]

In the first days of war the British were no better at camouflaging airfields than the French or Germans. RAF fields and facilities in Kent, just a few minutes' flying time from Luftwaffe airfields in occupied France, had been painted since 1939 – but

not very effectively. When German fighters and bombers came in the summer of 1940, the RAF fields were all pinpointed from pre-war information and easily located (photo 4-50). Lympne, just west of Folkstone, was not a British fighter station, but suffered a thorough hammering anyway. Neighbouring 11 Group fighter bases were similarly camouflaged and also got the 'full treatment' from Göring's eagles. The simplistic camouflage and the failure to tone down concrete roads and aircraft parking aprons made Lympne easy to see. False hedgerows on the grass landing ground never had a chance to disguise this field with its facilities remaining so prominent.[18]

Even at a newly expanded military airfield the hangars were usually the most dominant structures. They were easy to spot from the air and intelligence was very interested in them (photo 4-51). Activity around hangars could help identify the primary function of the field (by type of aircraft present) and the number of planes routinely in maintenance status gave an idea of the normal complement on the field.[19] The centre example on photo 4-51 shows

18. The light spots were filled-in bomb craters.

19. Many aircraft around hangars could mean a big raid was in the offing. It was much harder to count and measure activity in dispersed parking areas since these were more frequently camouflaged.

large hangars partially hidden and totally covered from observation. At the bottom of the same page is a small hangar that would have been exceptionally well hidden but for its stark white concrete apron.

Untoned concrete of ramps and taxiways frequently led the eye to unobtrusive hangars (photo 4-52). In the centre example on this photo, several aircraft parking shelters were caught in various stages of camouflage. At annotation 'A' a very well disguised shelter was identified by its taxiway and the shadow from its hangar roof. In the bottom example, four aircraft shelters (and more on either side) were well hidden by paint and netting. Note how much more effective the camouflage

became when the taxiways were painted a dulling colour.

At the German seaplane base at Tonning, draped nets and netting on moveable framework was used to completely change or hide the shape of airfield buildings (photo 4-53). Netting angled off the roof killed shadows and made buildings settle into their surroundings. Screens of nets shielded entrances from oblique observation. Netting was also used to alter the shape of roof lines (annotations C and D) (photo 4-54). A German tactical airfield in France used the same netting techniques seen at Tonning (photo 4-55). Heavy netting closed off hangar openings while real and fake trees and bushes

4-44 Photography of an airfield in northern Germany showed dispersed aircraft parking aligned with the local road pattern to make it less obvious. The airfield itself, the light area in photo centre, was also nicely toned to hide its function. British photo, 21 July 1943. Also note the double lines of barbed wire indicating a security installation (tailless arrows).

4-45 US photo of an airfield in southern Germany, 4 December 1944. Planes parked in widely dispersed revetments and hidden in the trees were given away by their taxiways.

4-46 British photography of Cambrai/Epinoy airfield, near Arras, France, probably in 1942. The Germans had built aircraft shelters looking like houses on the outskirts of the town. Taxiways were also supposed to blend into the town pattern.

HOUSE TYPE
CAMOUFLAGE

Fighter aircraft shelters (A), at EELDE (HOLLAND), in photograph to the left, have been camouflaged to resemble nearby houses (B).

Bomber aircraft shelters (A), in photograph to the right, have been camouflaged at LILLE/VENDEVILLE as groups of buildings round a courtyard and closely resembling genuine buildings of this type nearby (B). Position of some shelters is revealed by obvious taxi tracks (C).

Bomber aircraft shelters (A), at CORMEILLES-en-VEXIN, camouflaged as single villas with painted gardens, but too large to match the genuine houses (B). Other shelters (C) covered with darkened netting and dummy bushes to merge with patches of wood.

4-47 Page from a British intelligence report on camouflaged German airfields. The top example is good, the centre made too obvious by the taxiways and the bottom example was an excellent camouflage effort.

4-48 *German airfield near L'Orient, France, 8 June 1944. Some of the taxiways and shelters were toned down, but most taxiways were too obvious. Some of the large aircraft shelters had ineffective painted camouflage.*

4-49 *At a major civil airfield it was usually a waste of time to put camouflage on a 'hangar row'. French camouflage at Le Bourget Aerodrome on a British photo taken after German occupation, 1940.*

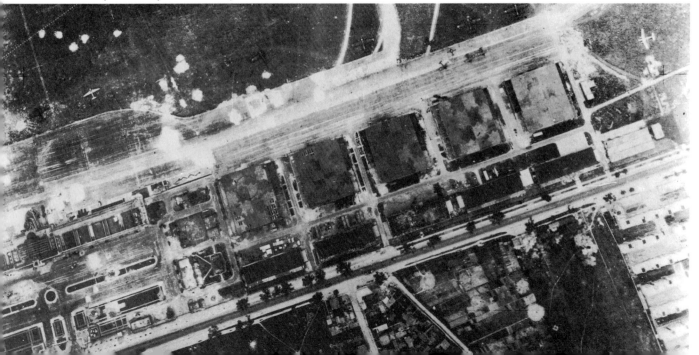

4-50 British pre-war camouflage of well known airfields did not hide the buildings nor deter German bombing. Despite camouflage, four of six large hangars have been destroyed at RAF Lympne, in SE England. A German reconnaissance plane took this photo in September 1940. Note how the grass landing ground was crossed by tar lines intended to look like hedgerows.

studded building roofs. It was all designed to make the structures appear as wooded hills. Even a control tower got the net and tree treatment.

Simulating trees to hide a roof was a standard camouflage technique in the late 1930s. A lot of work went into using nets to construct bogus forests – most of it wasted because the camouflage was not carried on beyond the buildings themselves. One British attempt was coupled with random pattern disruptive painting (photo 4-56). Once again, the white concrete apron in front of the building spoiled the effect. A close look at the heavily garnished nets peaked to simulate pine forests shows how simple they were to create (photo 4-57). These shapes not only looked good in direct observation but they would also cast convincing shadows. The square shape of the control tower required different trees and a drape of netting.

The Poles simulated taller trees using tepee-like frames covered with netting in their camouflage of Rakow airfield, south of Warsaw (photo 4-58).[20]

Nets connected adjacent hangars and each roof was dotted with the fake trees. The whole effect was intended to appear like wooded hills. Strip netting angled far out from the hangars in front and behind so the 'hills' gradually rose to hangar roof peak height (photo 4-59). Additional netting hills were raised at different places around the landing ground to permit covered parking of aircraft. Apparently the camouflage was not completed when war began in 1939 as some of the hangars in the distance remained uncovered. Detail of the Polish camouflage shows use of plain and garnished netting in addition to the strip nets in photo 4-59 (photo 4-60).

Hills would have been inappropriate at many airfields, so urban camouflage was another favourite choice. Making hangars look like rows of houses required altering the appearance of roof lines and adjacent parking aprons. As usual, good work on hangars was frequently spoiled by inattention to the adjacent concrete. An example of this was at Antwerp (photo 4-61). In the centre example on photo 4-61, outstanding construction on hangar roofs at Liege really looked like houses but

20. The photos of Rakow were taken after German occupation.

the parking apron was crudely marked. Perhaps the lines were guides for a more elaborate paint job as yet uncompleted. In any case, as the contemporary British Intelligence report points out, this airfield was in open country and the 'houses' were out of place.[21]

Like most camouflage, hangars disguised as rows of houses looked better from the ground than from

the air (photo 4-62). Camouflage such as this was in place at several British airfields just before the war began in earnest. It appears that the grass landing ground was untouched by any disguise.

Landing Ground Toning
Finding an undisguised grass landing ground from the air was child's play (photo 4-63). Normal land use (certainly in Europe) never kept such large spaces flat and open, uncrossed by roads or streams. Indeed, under peacetime conditions the

21. In the bottom example, several versions of dazzle paint patterns were used to kill shadows at the German field at Villacoublay, France.

4-51 Page from a British report on German airfield camouflage. The centre example was crude, but would deny intelligence a look at what was going on. Except for the undarkened concrete, camouflage in the bottom example was quite good.

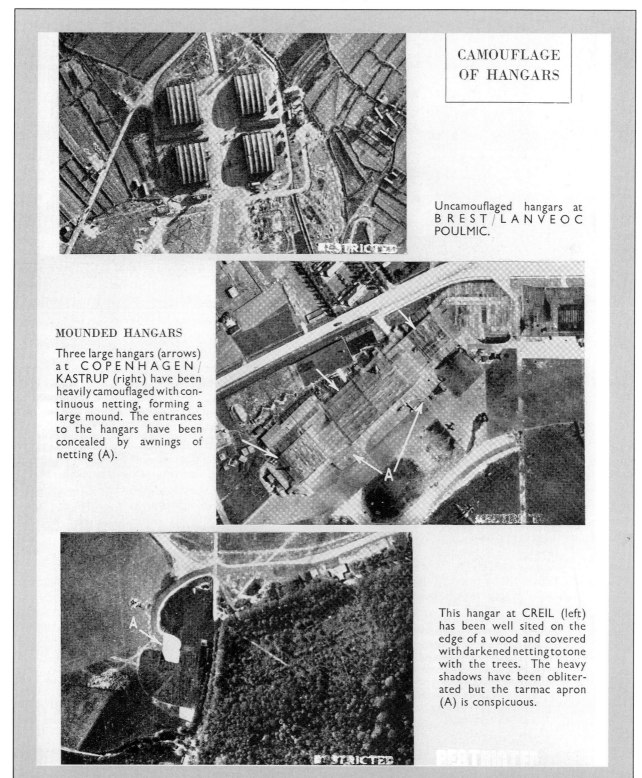

CAMOUFLAGE OF HANGARS

Uncamouflaged hangars at BREST/LANVEOC POULMIC.

MOUNDED HANGARS

Three large hangars (arrows) at COPENHAGEN/ KASTRUP (right) have been heavily camouflaged with continuous netting, forming a large mound. The entrances to the hangars have been concealed by awnings of netting (A).

This hangar at CREIL (left) has been well sited on the edge of a wood and covered with darkened netting to tone with the trees. The heavy shadows have been obliterated but the tarmac apron (A) is conspicuous.

object was to make a landing ground easy for an airman to locate. The example is a German photo of RAF West Malling, south-east of London near Sevenoaks. This airfield was new as an RAF base and the new ground scarring for military facilities made light tones that increased the field's visibility.[22] The most prominent scars came from the new heart-shaped perimeter taxiway which was needed for all-weather operations.[23]

Previous examples have shown how an undisguised landing ground could destroy the effectiveness of facilities' camouflage. The converse was also true. Mockau airfield at Leipzig was a good case in point. The field itself was well disrupted by

patterns on the grass that made it blend into the field patterns around it (photo 4-64). Undisguised hangars and parking aprons ruined the camouflage effect and made Mockau easy to see.

---

22. West Malling had been a civil airfield until June 1940. At the time of photo 4-63, the field had already been bombed five times. The only RAF unit present on 7 September 1940 was Number 26 Squadron, an Army Co-operation unit equipped with Lysanders. Apparently the Luftwaffe did not know which RAF units were where – they were simply attacking every airfield they knew about.

23. Building a well drained taxiway was essential because grass was so slippery when wet.

4-52 Another page from the British report on camouflage. The centre example shows how a shadow could ruin good camouflage. Netting camouflage in the bottom example was excellent.

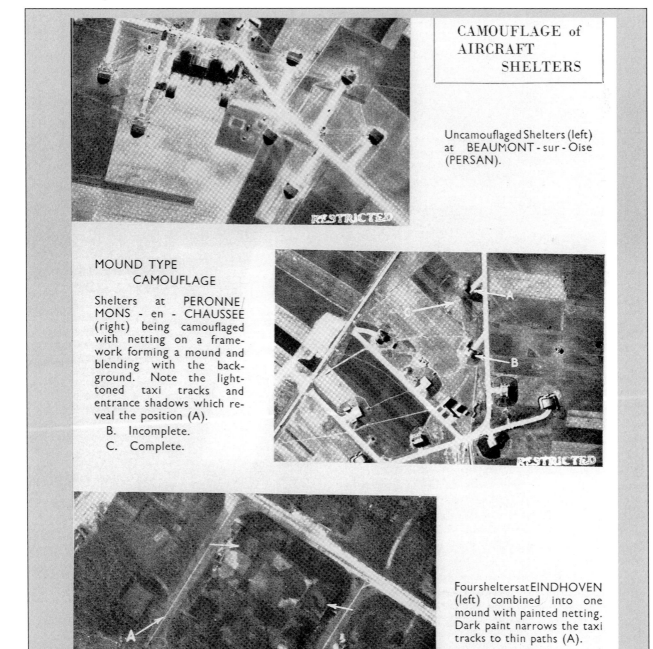

CAMOUFLAGE of AIRCRAFT SHELTERS

Uncamouflaged Shelters (left) at BEAUMONT - sur - Oise (PERSAN).

MOUND TYPE CAMOUFLAGE

Shelters at PERONNE/ MONS - en - CHAUSSEE (right) being camouflaged with netting on a frame-work forming a mound and blending with the back-ground. Note the light-toned taxi tracks and entrance shadows which re-veal the position (A).

B. Incomplete.
C. Complete.

Four shelters at EINDHOVEN (left) combined into one mound with painted netting. Dark paint narrows the taxi tracks to thin paths (A).

4-53 *Oblique view of the use of nets at the German Tonning seaplane base. Netting was draped to kill shadows, mask the hangar opening, and break up the roof line.*

4-54 *An olive drab B-17 hidden under an arched framework covered with heavily garnished chicken-wire. Hoevett Field, Mareeba, Australia, 21 November 1942. (DAVA, USArmy)*

4-55 *(Below right) Elaborate use of net and garnish camouflage by the Germans at an occupied airfield in France, 4 July 1943. The nets masking the hangar were augmented by fake and real bushes and trees.*

A comparison of before and after a fairly good integrated camouflage effort serves to demonstrate the necessity for blending both landing area and facilities into their background (photos 4-65 and 4-66). In a 1940 photo the roofs of two large hangars showed amateurish disruptive painting, but other buildings, the paved parking apron and roads were unmistakable. One year later, in 1941, the field, apron and hangars had all been painted to break up their lines and shadows. Clearly there was more to be done on the roads and smaller buildings but this camouflage would probably have been reasonably effective as is.

A really effective job of toning down a grass landing ground occurred at Bickendorf airfield near Köln, Germany (photo 4-67). The circular field was turned into a series of diagonal farm fields divided by a country road. This camouflage worked because airfield buildings had also been darkened, though there was room for improvement on the structures.

4-56 Pre-war British camouflage of a hangar with disruptive paint pattern supplemented by heavily garnished nets peaked to simulate small pine trees.

4-57 Control tower at the British installation in photo 4-56, showing construction of the fake trees.

4-58 A different and surprisingly good simulation of pine trees with netting. Polish camouflage at Rakow airfield south of Warsaw. German photo from 1939 after they occupied the airfield.

4-59 Another German photo of the Polish camouflage in photo 4-58. Large sections of strip nets angling gradually to the ground precluded shadows. The flaw was that the field itself remained too obvious.

4-60 Detail of Polish netting at Rakow airfield south of Warsaw, German photo, 1939.

Another approach to hiding an airfield in open country was to simulate hedgerows, streams, ditches, fence lines or other obstructions to make the clear landing surface seem to be broken into segments too small to land aircraft. The only limitation to this technique was that camouflage markings on a landing ground had to be flat so they did not interfere with airfield operations.[24] This eliminated a number of camouflage possibilities, leaving only toning or similar ground marking that had no actual three dimensional impact.[25] Considering the available options, airfield camouflage became a simple matter. Paint, stain, oil, cinders, or burning the grass could all be used to darken sections of a sod landing ground (photo 4-68).

Like other camouflage, to be effective marked grass fields had to be maintained. This required a great deal of work since use of a field tended to wear camouflage off the grass quickly (photo 4-69). What camouflage was not worn off by aircraft tyres would be covered or altered as the grass grew,

demanding periodic retoning of the field. At RAF Tern Hill, a bomber base 35 miles south-east of Liverpool, what was once a good simulation of hedgerows had been badly worn away by September 1940. Heavy activity by taxying planes and alert vehicles had left long streaks on the field and sections of the bogus hedgerows were rubbed away. At least the hangars, and a number of other airfield facilities, were camouflaged to make it harder for the Luftwaffe to find Tern Hill.

Flaws in Tern Hill's camouflage were readily apparent when the field was seen in its overall context (photo 4-70). German photos of Tern Hill prove that the Luftwaffe could not have been deceived by this camouflage. Surrounding fields had a decidedly clean, neat look when compared with the field. Bombers parked in the fields surrounding the landing ground required a second look to locate but were definitely visible. Another give-away was to note where hedgerows had been breached to permit planes access to dispersed parking in neighbouring fields. The decoy aircraft positioned in the open or painted on dark splotches on the grass, were all too obvious (see photo 4-15 for enlargement). The decoys were also too remote from the field to be believable, nor did they have a clear path to taxi to the field.

The Germans put together a really good landing ground camouflage at their field near Alkmar, 17 miles north of Amsterdam. Realistic dummy ditches were painted on the grass field and the limited facilities were effectively toned down. One of the best techniques used was the well executed continuation of surrounding field, road, and ditch lines onto the field itself. This deception was given away when a British photoreconnaissance plane

---

24. Three dimensional moveable obstructions were occasionally used but these had two disadvantages at an active field. First, they had to be moved each time the airfield was in use and replaced in precisely the same location or their displacement would disclose the field. Second, the act of moving the obstructions could leave marks on the ground that broke the camouflage discipline.

25. Simulation of three dimensional obstructions was vulnerable to stereo viewing of aerial photos. The Allies did nearly all photo interpretation using stereo viewing techniques. The Germans and Japanese used stereo only in later, and special, phases of photo-intelligence work. This meant that Allied two dimensional camouflage was relatively more effective than similar work by the Axis nations.

4-61 From the air, hangars could be made to look like rows of houses — but only if taxiways and parking aprons were equally well disguised. From a British report on airfield camouflage.

caught the field one frosty morning in February 1941 (photo 4-71). Light snow covered the landscape and real ditches were frozen over, showing white. The fake ditches of the camouflage remained dark, making the landing ground stand out against its background.

Sometimes nature helped camouflage a landing ground. A Japanese field that had pre-empted space in Chinese rice paddies was made harder to see from a distance when the ancient field boundaries bled through to tone the surface (photo 4-72). Stark, undisguised parking aprons, taxiways and revetments prove that this camouflage was unintentional.

4-62 Ground view of British hangars disguised as housing rows in pre-war camouflage. As usual the field itself was not camouflaged to the same standard.

Paved Runway Painting

Airfields with paved runways presented the dual problem of blending the hard surfaces with adjacent grass, and then blending both into the surrounding countryside. The key was to disrupt the long straight lines of the paved runways. A related and perhaps more difficult challenge was to hide runway intersections as these tended to stand out in sharp contrast to any shapes found in nature.

RAF Tangmere, three miles east of the Roman camp city of Chichester, had runways camouflaged as well as any in the early days of war (photo 4-73). Tangmere was a long-established British military airfield going back to 1917. Its grass field had been converted to an all-weather fighter base between 1937 and 1939. There was no question that the Germans knew where the field was and that it was a primary target.[26] In July 1940 Tangmere was given a satellite grass field at Westhampnett. The lightly used emergency field was camouflaged with tar to simulate hedgerows and stands up to close examination – even when you know where to look. German intelligence probably did not know about the satellite field.[27]

Tangmere itself was in a bad position for camouflage. The characteristic Chichester by-pass road was undisguised. Easily located, even at night, the road was like a pointer aimed at the airfield. Still, the field had to be protected by camouflage and the work was well done. Concrete runways were nicely toned down and blended with the surrounding field pattern. At the time of the German photo taken on 12 August 1940, the Tangmere camouflage was broken by failure to darken the circling taxiway.[28]

Most runway camouflage was far from successful. One Japanese field near Shanghai was painted by men who obviously had never seen the

4-63 Finding an uncamouflaged grass airfield from the air was no trick as shown by this 7 September 1940 German photo of RAF West Malling in Kent.

26. The field had been known as a fighter base for years. Three squadrons of Hurricanes were stationed at Tangmere when the shooting war started.

27. Tangmere got a second satellite field at Merston in 1941 (single arrow).

28. Tangmere was first bombed three days after photo 4-73 was taken. By mid-September the taxiway was also camouflaged.

4-64 Just as an easily found airfield negated good camouflage of the facilities, undisguised hangars could disclose a well toned-down landing ground. British photo of Leipzig/Mockau airfield, 3 October 1941.

earth from the air (photo 4-74). Another Japanese airfield, Atsugi south-west of Tokyo, showed dazzle patterns that did nothing to break up the lines of the runways (photo 4-75).[29] Spotted camouflage was used by the Japanese at a second airfield near Shanghai (photo 4-76). In this case, the unnatural pattern did not blend well with surrounding paddies, but was still less obvious than the uncamouflaged connecting taxiways. The same Japanese field more than a year later showed that new runways and revetments were uncamouflaged while the unique spotted paint work had clearly been maintained (photo 4-77). Mottled camouflage on a Japanese runway near Wuchang, China, worked fairly well where the pattern was fine grained (photo 4-78). The large pattern mottle paint work actually called attention to the field.

Simple darkening of runway edges in an irregular pattern tended to obscure the straight lines where the painted tone matched its background (photo 4-79). This technique was used at the German airfield near Lorient, France, in 1944. Where the paint and background tones did not match, the effect was to outline the runway. In addition, the simulated roads should have been continued through the grass areas or not used at all.

At times a few lines in the right place produced a good level of camouflage. The German airfield at Wismer was near the coast and easy for a bomber to find with its three runways showing clearly. The field was disguised in 1943 with toned-down

runways. The addition of a few parallel lines and irregular shapes served to disrupt the runway intersections (photo 4-80). At short range the Wismer camouflage was nothing special, but it was much better from a bomber's perspective (photo 4-81).

At first glance strong rectangular patterns might disguise a runway, but, like dazzle patterns, long straight lines violate what is expected in nature (photo 4-82). Toning an airfield in large blocks of drab colours might keep a casual observer from noticing the installation. Even when well done, large rectangular patterns could not hide a runway if attention was called to the area. This was never more true than when the airfield was in close proximity to undisguised landmarks. A prime example was the British airfield at Haifa, Palestine (now Israel) as seen on a German photo. The runways were toned down and hard to see, but a bomber could have hit the field without ever seeing it (photo 4-83). Anyone with a map could have intersected lines between the river, the oil storage tank farm and the coast to locate the airfield.

An urban setting demanded urban camouflage on the runway. The Boeing runway at Seattle, Washington, was dressed up as a series of city blocks (photo 4-84). The adjacent factory, making B-17s, was hidden under paint and nets using the same city block pattern. It was almost impossible to pick out the runway itself, but no one needed to. The river and railway nicely bracket the installation so this airfield was simple to locate from overhead.

Fake Damage
Another way to protect a runway was to accept that the location could not be disguised and to make it look like the installation was damaged beyond use.

---

29. Atsugi was where General Douglas MacArthur first landed in Japan when he came to accept surrender. This photo was taken after the Japanese had surrendered but before the formal ceremony. The piles of planes were Japanese; the plane on the taxiway was a US C-47 transport.

Unrepaired bomb craters would also indicate a lack of interest and therefore a lack of activity. The Germans tried the fake crater dodge several times with little success. Even well painted craters lacked realistic shadows. More telling was the absence of the delicate star patterns of a real blasted hole in concrete (photo 4-85). Some fake craters were so crude that they seem almost humorous (photo 4-86). In both examples nearby real craters not only serve for comparison, but prove that Allied airmen were not fooled.

Decoy Airfields

Like every other class of major installation, really important airfields were not only camouflaged but protected by decoys. The effort and cost to make a decoy were worth it if they confused even a few bomb-aimers and caused a few loads to go astray. Some decoy airfields were imaginative and elaborate.

Many airfield decoys were designed against night bombers and, as such, did not require much detail. One of the best ploys was to mount a dummy plane on a rail so it could be moved rapidly to simulate a take off or landing (photo 4-87). The plane would be supplied with landing lights and the 'runway' with the typical lights of a flarepath. Simulated hangars would be 'careless' in their use of lights, as would parties working on other dummy aircraft. In fact the whole decoy complex would be run by a few men manning the lights and landing rail from a nearby bomb-proof bunker.

4-65 Camouflage was total or it was useless. Paint on the roof of these RAF hangars achieved nothing. British photo is captioned 'No. 2 Area Seletar, 28 October 1940' (The only Seletar I know of is at Singapore)

4-66 A year after photo 4-65 the airfield and its facilities were nicely blended into their surroundings. Though still visible on photography, a night raider would have found the field hard to find. British photo, 21 October 1941.

4-67 A well-toned grass field at Köln/Bickendorf. Different sections of the field were coloured to resemble farm fields. The British caption states that this airfield was camouflaged three different ways in nine months.

4-68 Grass fields could be quickly disguised using tar, oil, or simply burning the grass, to simulate hedgerows, orchards or other obstacles. US Army Engineers spreading kerosene to burn grass during manoeuvres in Louisiana, September 1941. (National Archives)

4-69 (Right) A grass landing ground could be made to pose as a series of fields divided by hedgerows or fence lines – but the camouflage had to be maintained. RAF Tern Hill, German photo, 27 September 1940. See photos 4-14 and 4-70.

GX 10331/898a/40 SD   v. 27.9.40.

4-70 The Tern Hill camouflage was not too impressive when seen in its overall context. German photo, 27 September 1940. Note the parking of actual aircraft just off the field, and decoys at some distance.

4-71 German camouflage of Alkmar airfield, Netherlands. Outstanding marking of the field with fake ditches was given away when the RAF photographed the field on 16 February 1941. Real ditches showed white with ice and dummy ditches were still dark.

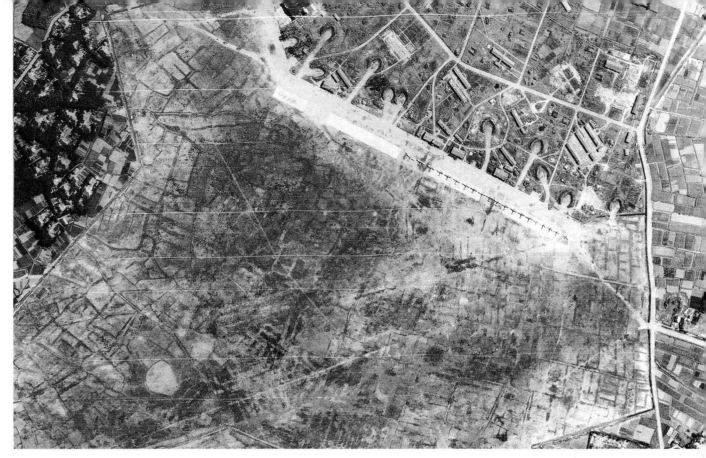

4-72 *Nature helped camouflage a Japanese airfield in China when the earlier paddy field pattern showed through. US photo, 20 September 1945.*

4-73 *RAF Tangmere east of Chichester, England. The crossing runways were well camouflaged but exposed by the circling taxiway. The main and satellite fields are marked by arrows (see footnotes 27 and 28). German photo, 12 August 1940.*

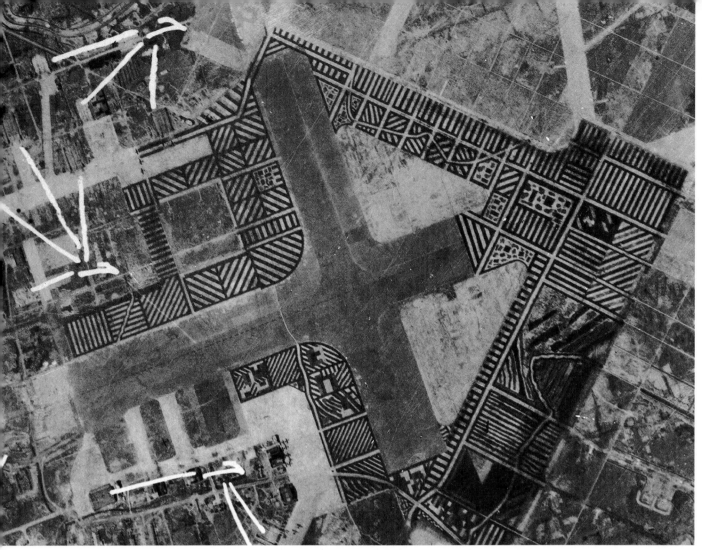

4-74 *Runway camouflage was often more fanciful than useful. US photo of Japanese Kiangwan Airfield, Shanghai, 1945. World War II annotations show parking revetments.*

4-75 *Dazzle paint patterns on the Atsugi runway, south-west of Tokyo. US photo, 29 August 1945.*

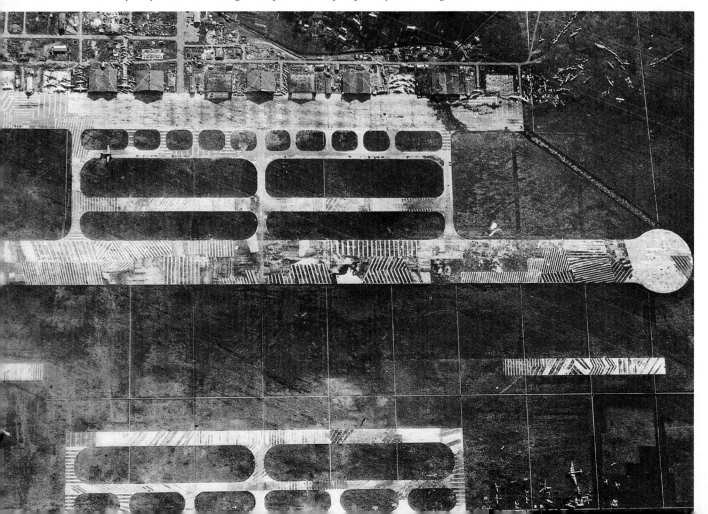

4-76 Unique Japanese spotted runway camouflage at Tachang Airfield near Shanghai. US photo, 5 October 1943.

4-77 Tachang Airfield in 1945. A new runway and revetments were added but not camouflaged. For some reason the old runway paint scheme was maintained.

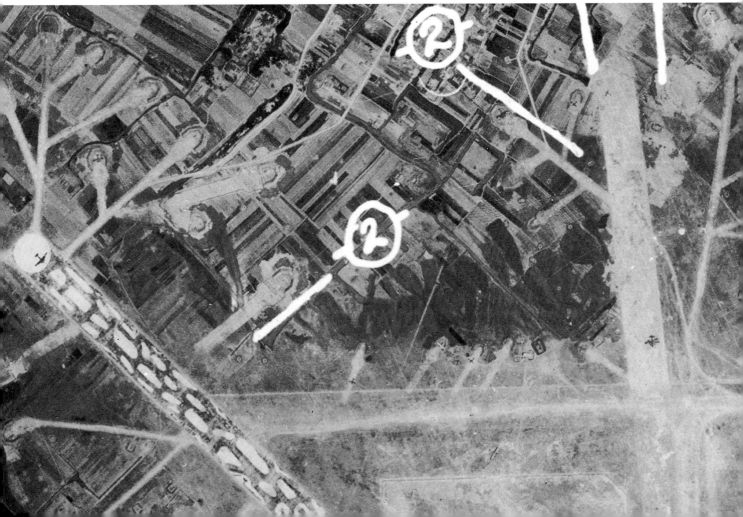

4-78 A strange mottled paint pattern on the Japanese airfield at Wuchang, China. US photo, 31 March 1943.

4-79 Paint designed to disrupt the long straight edges of a concrete runway. US photo of the German field at L'Orient, France, 8 June 1944.

With proper lighting, a credible night decoy airfield could be achieved with a few lines. Little detail was required beyond a few characteristic shapes that would be visible to the night raider overhead (photo 4-88). Day decoys, on the other hand, had to be completely filled out with all the shapes and facilities an airman would expect to see at an airfield (photo 4-89). Both of these German airfield decoy examples from France had one thing in common – they did not work. There is not a bomb crater in sight. The first, once found in the day time and recorded on maps, would find few takers from night bomber crews who paid attention to their intelligence briefings. The second was too clean and too obviously plunked down on top of a road and field pattern that it did not interrupt. A real airfield would have rubber streaks and oil or fuel stains on the concrete. It would also have resulted in the road from the town being diverted around the end of the runway. Once it was identified, the value of a decoy field diminished considerably.

A reasonably good decoy airfield was built by the Germans near Karup airfield in central Denmark (photo 4-90). The fake hangars, taxiways and runway were easy to see but had the flavour of being toned down. This decoy was designed to look like an inept camouflage job that let the airfield show through. The whole effect was enhanced by

4-80 *The simple addition of a few lines crossing the orientation of runways and disrupting their intersections could produce a reasonable degree of camouflage. British photo of Wismer, Germany, 5 November 1943.*

clever use of dummy planes, lights and a take-off simulator. Note that despite the detail, there were no bomb craters around the Grove/Karup decoy.

Not all decoys were failures. Nordholz, north of Bremen near Cuxhaven, was a major threat to Allied bombing. It was in a position to launch night fighters against bombers from England heading for Kiel, Stettin or on a northern route to Berlin. In 1942 the airfield was toned down so its concrete did not show at night, but the field was not camouflaged in the strict sense of the word (photo 4-91). When a US photo plane covered Nordholz in June 1943 the lines of the field had been disrupted with paint and stain (photo 4-92). Its facilities were still readily visible, but not nearly so much as a year earlier.

Three and a half miles closer to England sat the Nordholz decoy. It had the right runways and the right orientation (photo 4-93). Realistic hangars and oil storage tanks completed the scene. In 1942, the major flaws in this decoy were that it was too neat and clean, and the ladder-taxiway was straight, rather than curved on one end like the real field. By 1943 the decoy had been toned down, or neglected, but not too much to make it hard to see (photo 4-

94). The fake taxiways and hangars showed nicely, though the oil tanks were disappearing from view (arrow). This decoy was good enough to draw a few bombs away from the real airfield (tailless arrows).

The most perfectly camouflaged runways were not runways at all. In 1945, with Allied fighter-bombers roaming at will over German territory, no airfield was safe. The Luftwaffe began to operate fighters – including jets – from highway strips.[30] All that was required was to find a straight section of road sufficiently long to serve as a runway. The grass median would then be paved over to make a surface wide enough. Camouflage was essential to make the highway strip look like the median was still in place. American photo interpreters found one of these autobahn airstrips by spotting aircraft revetments in a location where they did not belong (photo 4-95). The price for being caught was predictable (photo 4-96).

---

30. Use of highways as war-emergency landing strips was later incorporated in operational doctrine of the US Strategic Air Command and provided part of the original justification for the massive US Defense and Interstate Highway System built from the 1950s on.

4-81 Wismer, Germany from a US reconnaissance plane at 28,000 feet, (8,600 m) 24 May 1944. Can you find the airfield in photo 4-80?

4-82 Attempts to blend a runway into a local field pattern might appear good at first glance, but usually failed because they retained some straight line orientation that showed runways. German airfield in France, 1942. Annotations show (A) camouflaged dispersal areas (B) a new dispersal under construction.

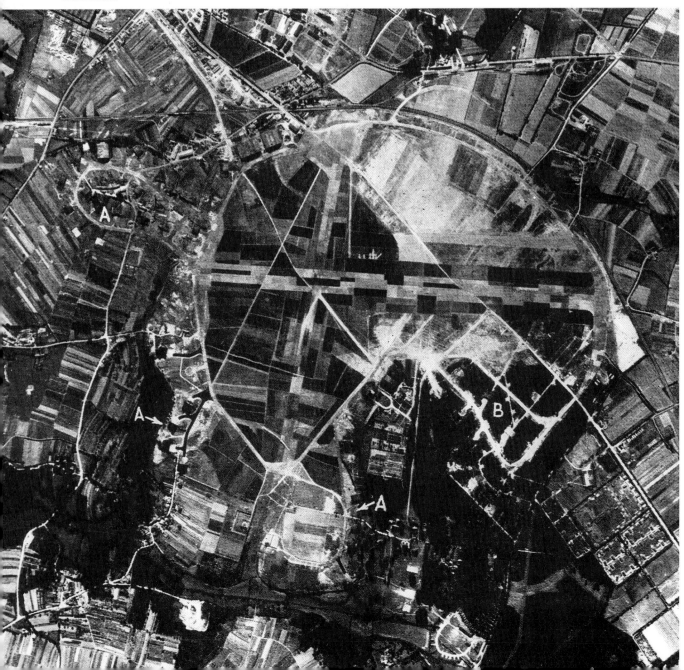

4-83 Relative positioning of an airfield was as important as camouflage. Some, such as Haifa, Palestine (now Israel), were located between landmarks that negated much of the value of their camouflage. The coast, river, and oil storage tank farm clearly bracketed the runways. German photo, 4 August 1942.

4-84 An urban setting demanded different styles of camouflage paint work. Boeing plant at Seattle, Wash., as it looked on 28 August 1943. B-17s parked at lower right show the line of the runway. Arrows show the camouflaged factory with more bombers parked just outside.

4-85 Painted craters (arrows) simulated a runway that could not be used, but did not save this German airfield from getting more real ones (tailless arrow). The real craters had shadows. Also note the interesting painted camouflage on several hangars. British photo, 28 May 1944.

4-86 An example of crude fake bomb craters on a thoroughly bombed airfield in southern Germany. British photo, 29 May 1944.

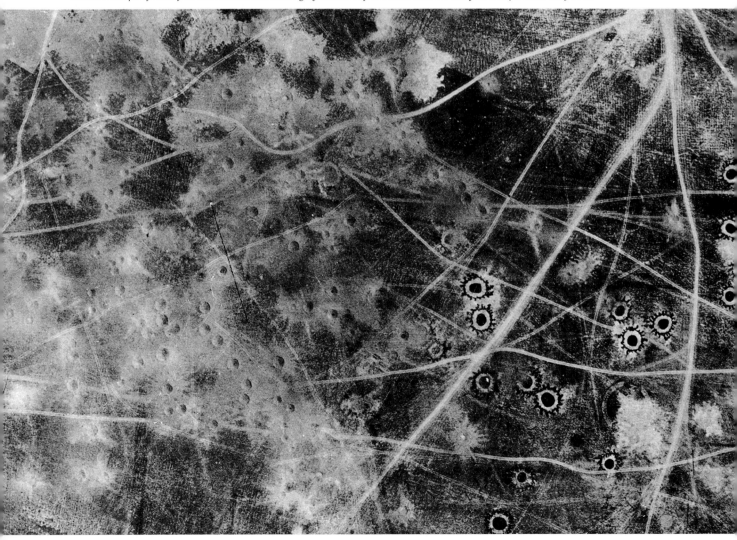

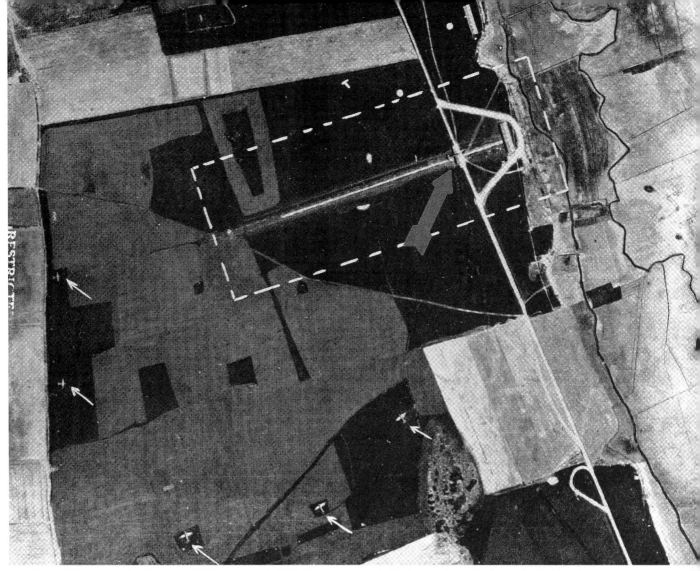

4-87 *German Herning/Sunds night decoy airfield in Denmark, 1942. The outlined area held a dummy aircraft (arrow) on a rail designed to simulate landings after dark. Contemporary annotations (tailless arrows) indicate other dummy planes. The absence of bomb craters proves that this decoy did not work.*

4-88 *Night decoy airfields did not require a lot of detail, a few lines and lights were deemed sufficient. The absence of bomb craters in the area indicates decoy failure. British photo of the German Lannion/Kerprigent airfield in France, 8 March 1942.*

Possible Take-Off Device

Dummy H

4-89 *The German Vannes/Grandchamp day decoy airfield in France, was too obvious – and too clean – to be real. British photo, 8 February 1942.*

4-90 *Grove/Karup, Denmark, was a well done German decoy airfield complete with a fake take-off device, dummy planes, hangars and taxiways. British photo, 26 June 1943.*

4-91 *Nordholz airfield near Bremen with triangle runways toned down. British photo, 1942.*

4-92 *Nordholz airfield after camouflage, US photo, 13 June 1943.*

4-93 *Three and a half miles south of Nordholz was a well detailed decoy complete with fake oil tanks, revetments, taxiways, and buildings (compare with photo 4-91). British photo, 1942.*

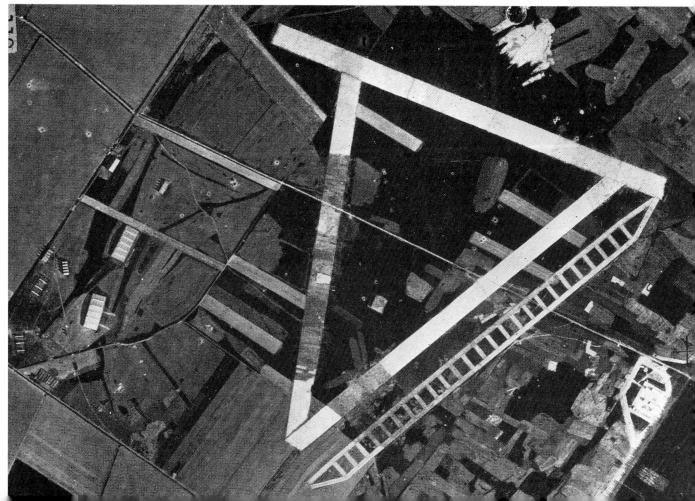

4-94 The Nordholz decoy after it had been made less obvious. The fake oil tanks were not being kept up (arrow), but US bombers fell for the decoy anyway (tailless arrows show bomb-craters). US photo, 13 June 1943.

4-95 A nearly perfectly camouflaged runway – a strip of autobahn with the grass median paved and darkened to look like it was still two strips of concrete. In March 1945, US photo interpreters spotted the aircraft revetments that gave this 'airstrip' away.

4-96 The price of camouflage failure. A German Me262 jet in a revetment next to a highway strip runway.

CHAPTER 5

TELL-TALE ARTERIES

Lines of Communication – Railways and Canals

Line-of-communications targets were as hard to hide as naval targets and for the same reasons. Although linear, they were massive in scale with locations generally well known from pre-war days and obvious in their environment. The way they crossed rivers and valleys, even dominant cultural features of the landscape were absolutely predictable. To make matters worse for a defender, transportation rights-of-way were not only targets themselves but they also sprawled over the landscape like signposts leading to other targets. Canals, roads and railway lines converge on the cities and factories like pointers (photo 5-1). An approaching bomber could usually pick up one of these characteristic arteries – even at night or in bad weather – and be led to their junction. Following a canal or railway line to a characteristic junction might help a lost aircrew find their way to some other distant target.

Short of permanently covering an entire country with netting or smoke, it was impossible to hide lines of communication. The best that could be done was to make key transportation segments or centres and equipment harder to find. If key transportation elements could not be completely disguised, then they might at least be made more difficult to identify or harder to see to bomb. No camouflage of lines of communication was effective against scrutiny of aerial photographs.

Roads

In populated areas of the world like Europe, road networks are so dense that trying to deal them a serious blow with aerial bombing is a waste of time. Certain 'choke points', such as bridges, tunnels or narrow passes are of course more vulnerable. However, most road damage can be either easily repaired or by-passed by simply driving around it or taking an alternate route. Further, few of the critical points on a road network lend themselves to camouflage and at the outset of hostilities they were too well known from before the war and too obvious in relation to other things that could not be hidden (photo 5-2). A major road bridge over a river could not be hidden because the river could not be made to disappear.

Even though the largest bridges were naturally the most critical and vulnerable points in a network, defenders recognised the futility of trying to camouflage a major bridge. The most significant bridges were protected by barrage balloons and anti-aircraft guns rather than camouflage (photo 5-3).

Areas of the world that were less populated than Western Europe had fewer paved roads and less well developed road networks. In these areas, road damage was frequently even easier to by-pass – usually by the simple expedient of driving around the bomb craters. Underdeveloped road networks did not camouflage well – even had there been a reason to make the effort.

The final factor making road camouflage a rare thing was that in 1939-45, truck and car travel was nothing like it is today in volume. Other means of transportation, mainly rail, carried the bulk of land cargo. During World War II the road target was not the road itself, but rather the vehicles thereon. In most cases on the continent of Europe, in North Africa, or in Asia during that era, vehicles on the roads would be either military or hauling a war related cargo. In those days, airmen considered anything moving fair game and trucks were easy to strafe. For this reason cars and trucks were camouflaged with paint or natural materials, but the camouflage was only effective when the vehicle was parked (photo 5-4).

Railways

The most numerous targets related to transportation were rail associated. Heavy and bulky cargo moved fastest on rails. Railways were heavily used to move tanks, troops, fuel and all the other resources of war. In Europe, rail networks were highly developed and extensive and therefore difficult to interdict since there were so many alternatives. Railways were rare in Eastern Europe, Africa and the Pacific, thus all the more conspicuous and vulnerable since there were fewer alternatives. Because of their relative scarcity when compared to road networks, railways were often themselves prime targets. In Europe, where rail lines and connections were well developed, a significant break in a carefully selected 'choke point' on a major rail line could still prove difficult to repair, causing massive backups in freight or military movements. In the rest of the world experiencing combat, rail systems were so sparse and primitive that it was not necessary to locate key points to destroy. Outside Europe, rail rights-of-way were so vulnerable they could be effectively attacked at any point along their length.

Rail traffic in Europe was the key to Axis industrial health as well as military mobility and flexibility. Being among the most highly developed rail systems in the world was a mixed blessing for

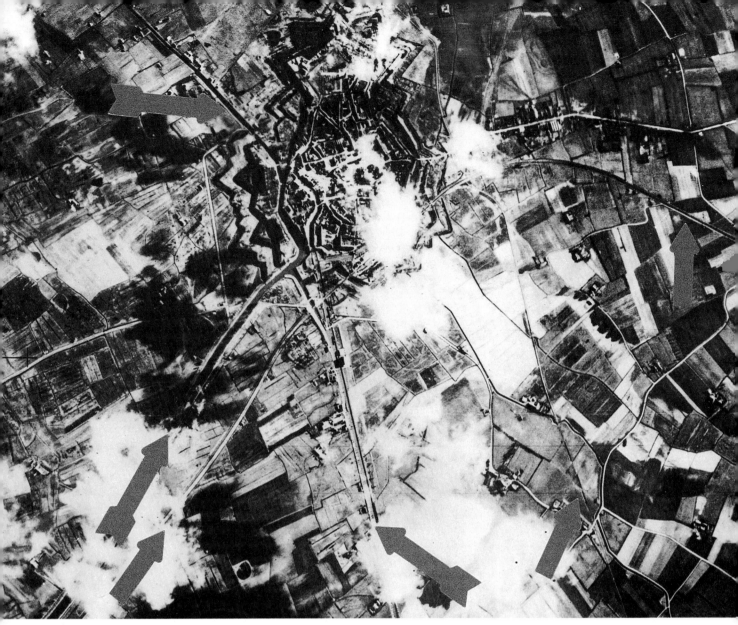

5-1 Roads, canals and railways were often effective pointers to lead airmen to other navigation landmarks and targets. Arrows indicate canals, tailless arrows show railways. Bergues, Belgium, from a British photo of 10 February 1941.

5-2 Rhine River road bridge near Wesel, Germany, pre-war photo (circa 1931).

5-3 Barrage balloons defended the Rhine River bridge at Wesel, Germany, 12 September 1945. There were at least 20 barrage balloons protecting this bridge.

5-4 Japanese staff cars in China, 1938. The car on the left was painted a neutral light brown; the other car had a camouflage pattern paint scheme.

Europe. The widespread rail networks that offered many alternative routes also offered a large number of vulnerable junctions and choke points as targets. Rail lines were also essential to connect key industrial targets with raw materials and depot destinations. Therefore rail lines could be counted upon to betray better hidden, higher priority objectives (see Chapter 6).

Of course, railway rolling stock and equipment was also a prime target for airmen, with locomotives being especially hard to replace. A parked train carefully camouflaged on a remote siding might escape notice from passing aircrews, but a moving train was terribly obvious (photo 5-5). Camouflaged or not, a moving train – particularly a steam engine – could be spotted miles away from the air. It was not entirely smoke and steam that gave trains away, though these certainly made an attacking airman's job much easier (photo 5-6). From the air, a moving train was a slug of tonal difference breaking the normally long clean lines of a railbed (photo 5-7). Unless it was unusually well camouflaged and positioned, stationary railway equipment was equally easy to see. Fighter-bomber pilots normally had a field day when they were turned loose on rail lines (photo 5-8). Even when seen from high overhead, the varied colours and tones of uncamouflaged rail cars made them stand out against the background of gravel railbed in yards or out on the line (photo 5-9). The job of finding railway cars and equipment was made even easier when snow cover provided a smooth background for shadows (photo 5-10).

Though trains themselves were inherently vulnerable and nearly impossible to hide, attempts were often made to disguise key railway assets from attack. Bridges were a class of railway structure that got a great deal of attention from both attackers and defenders. As fixed location points of critical vulnerability for a rail line, bridges were frequently camouflaged despite their known locations in an attempt to make them harder for a fast moving plane to hit. Rail bridges were a more logical subject for camouflage than road bridges because they were more critical to networks and harder to hit and destroy (narrower and with a more open structure).

The most typical camouflage for a bridge was a draping of natural material (photo 5-11). Casting strong, unnatural shadows, the only virtue of this camouflage was toning the target to blend better with its surroundings. The natural material technique was even tried on moderately large bridges, with questionable success (photo 5-12). Since the roadbed was a clean, light-toned line, making a bridge look like a continuation of tree cover would only serve to attract attention to the structure. In any case, the river and rail line had to intersect with a bridge so pilots had no trouble finding these targets. The intersection principle negated camouflage of major rail bridges just as it did for road bridges.

5-5 A well-camouflaged train parked on a side track might escape notice, but a moving train – never. Burma, 1944.

5-6 A moving train as seen by a low-flying fighter-bomber. Belgium, 20 January 1943. Note the German machine gunner on the roof firing at the RAF plane.

Other railway structures frequently given camouflage attention were yard buildings and passenger stations. This was not because those facilities were pointers to other targets, though they were often collocated with targets like marshalling yards. The intent was to keep critical railway facilities from becoming the focus of an attack themselves. Trackage, small bridges, and even switches could be replaced relatively easily. Replacing the complex levers and electrical circuits of an interlocking switch or signal system was much more difficult.

Most railway yard buildings had scant clearance between their walls and the nearest tracks. This compounded the camouflage problem. With elaborate construction impractical, the work narrowed down to a paint job (photo 5-13). Simple disruptive patterns were used to make key buildings a little harder to identify. Where track clearance permitted, the camouflage solution would be a drape of garnished nets (photo 5-14). Neither paint nor nets alone would deter a bomber very long.

A major railway station was extremely difficult to camouflage. The building was large, the setting normally well supplied with approaching roads and broad open spaces for private and commercial vehicles. Of course, the incoming tracks were inescapable (photo 5-15). To make the problem worse, major railway terminals were frequently in close proximity to other easily identifiable landmarks, such as churches, bridges, or parks (photo 5-16). Finally, all of the major rail terminals were well known before the war and clearly marked on the maps of all the belligerents. The example used in photos 6-15 and 6-16 is Köln (Cologne), one of the best known stations in Europe. No attempt was made to camouflage Köln's main railway station because the nearby heavy iron trusses of the Hohenzollern Railway Bridge and the great cathedral were so well known and so obvious from the air.[1]

---

1. The cathedral, Hohenzollern Bridge and central railway station were key recognition points for both day and night bombers of the RAF. Köln was first bombed on 24/25 May 1940, two days before the Dunkirk evacuation began, and was attacked regularly throughout the war. It was here, on 30/31 May 1942 that the RAF made the first air attack with over a thousand bombers (1,046 aircraft were used). More than 18,000 dwellings and 600 acres of the city were destroyed.

5-7 Moving or stationary, the tonal differences of an uncamouflaged train against the railbed stood out like a sore thumb for both airmen and photo interpreters. Bergues, Belgium, 1944. Arrows show trains.

Despite a setting nearly as unique as at Köln, a very credible camouflage job was done on Hamburg's Dammtor Railway Station. Comparative photography showed Allied intelligence how the station was being disguised (photo 5-17). In the 'before' photo, the dual track rails passing through the station show clearly against their railbed as do the large open areas on either side of the station. The station itself cast strong shadows off both side and end. In the next photo, camouflaging had commenced (photo 5-18). A framework was erected over the big vehicle unloading area on one side on the station. The framework was covered with a material painted to resemble roads and topped with artificial trees. While the camouflaging was taking place, spring had brought out foliage and the camouflage was designed to match the natural scene. Sharp shadows still gave the station away but the material in place sloping to the ground cut off shadows on one side.

The third photo shows the Dammtor Station camouflage project completed (photo 5-19). Painted roads have been revised and simplified. Fake trees have been altered to look like the full foliage of summer. More important, the approaching tracks have been toned down and the roof of the station painted to look like another section of the rails. Another important detail was the extension of painted material from the other side of the station to the ground. This meant shadows were killed on both sides of the structure. The only serious flaws remaining were the shadow on one end – unavoidable if a train was to enter – and the small shadows of two entrances left in the new

5-8 Japanese tanks on flatcars found by Allied fighter-bombers. Burma, 1945.

camouflage material on the lower side of the station.

The following summer the Dammtor Station camouflage had undergone additional change (photo 5-20). Painted road patterns were gone except for the false grade crossing just to the left of the station. Sloping painted material still killed shadows on both sides of the building, but the end shadow was still a flaw. Approaching tracks were

5-9 Railway equipment showed clearly against a normal background of railbed. German photography of rail yards on the outskirts of Moscow, 1941.

5-10 Snow cover provided a background that made railway equipment or its shadows, even easier to see. German photography of Moscow, 1942.

5-11 *An industrious, but futile attempt to conceal a small railway bridge with natural materials. Burma, 1943.*

5-13 *Painted camouflage on a marshalling yard switch tower, Naples, Italy.*

5-12 *Natural camouflage for a rail bridge and pipeline. Burma, December 1943. Shadows easily give both structures away.*

5-14 *A simple railway station might be camouflaged by having its outline disrupted by nets. Berchtesgaden, Germany, 1945.*

toned down a considerable distance out from the station and the station camouflage theme was a dulling neutral colour. Were it not for the few unavoidable shadows and the characteristic open areas adjacent to the station, this camouflage job might be classed as very effective.

Camouflaging a marshalling yard was a more difficult challenge since the area to be disguised was usually very large. One of the better attempts was at Stuttgart. Paint was used to extend the surrounding road and building pattern out into the yard trackage (photo 5-21). The painted buildings were given reasonable painted shadows. Simple and effective, this camouflage might even have confused a bomb-aimer in daylight. It would surely have helped protect the yard during a night bombing raid.

Photo 5-21 also shows a nearby factory heavily painted to dull roofs, disguise large buildings and break up significant outlines. Further up and to the right is a well-camouflaged canal. Complete covering with material painted to look like buildings and grass made the 'L-shaped' canal difficult to pick out. It is probable that both the yard and canal were camouflaged to deny them as 'pointers' to the factory.

Later in the autumn or early the following spring, the Stuttgart camouflage exhibited change and some deterioration (photo 5-22). The paint in the yard had faded and not been renewed. Fake roads no longer extended down beyond the small bridge crossing the yard, though the earlier road pattern

still showed faintly. The factory had its paint renewed with the same basic patterns maintained but additional buildings camouflaged. Finally, the canal camouflage showed fading and was obviously not being refreshed. Weakness allowed to creep into the yard and canal camouflage work tend to confirm that the factory was the real objective all along.

Inland Waterways

Canals were every bit as difficult as railways to disguise. Europe had a well developed network of canals. They tended to stretch between major mining and industrial regions and ports to permit slow but very cheap movement of large volume bulk cargo such as coal, ores or steel ingots and girders. Like rail lines, canals could be traitorous pointers to key targets. Canals also had certain places where they were themselves extremely vulnerable. Particular points of vulnerability were where water in a canal could be spilled out. Locks at frequent intervals would limit such damage to an entire system, but a large segment of a canal could be drained by a few well placed, moderate sized bombs. Damage to a canal 'choke point' was not as easy to repair as a railway right-of-way.

Just as railway and highway bridges were the greatest points of potential harm on those systems, aqueducts were places were canals could be damaged most readily and most effectively. Aqueducts were the structures that allowed canals to cross roads, railways, rivers, valleys, or other

5-15 Aerial oblique of Köln, Germany, in March 1945. Smoke was from a recent air attack. The Köln Cathedral, Hohenzollern railway bridge, and the roof of the central railway station are clearly visible.

5-16 Vertical photograph of the area of photo 5-15, Köln, Germany, 5 August 1945. Light grey shows areas totally destroyed. Partially destroyed city blocks can be recognised by shells of walls from burned out houses. Major rail and highway bridges are down and a temporary road bridge has been installed by the Allies.

canals (photo 5-23). Damaging, let alone destroying, one of these structures not only incapacitated a section of canal but was difficult and expensive to repair, and unlike other lines of communication, had to be completely repaired before the canal could operate again.

One of the most travelled and most significant of Germany's inland waterways was the Dortmund-Ems Canal. Running north-south, this canal linked the biggest German inland port with the Ems River and thence to the North Sea (photo 5-24). It also connected with the Mittelland Canal which ran east from Rheine, Germany, to Berlin and the River Spree. Barges of up to 1,200 tons plied the main German canals. In addition to food, fuel and ore the canals were a major artery for bulk shipment of arms and ammunition.

A critical point along the Dortmund-Ems Canal occurred near Münster, where the waterway first crossed the Ems (upstream, before the river was barge navigable). The original Ems River aqueduct had been augmented by a new, wider aqueduct and both aqueducts were provided with guard locks. Even with protecting locks, a sudden air attack breaching the canal bank, or one of the aqueducts, could drain water from a considerable stretch of canal before the locks could be closed. If the breach

was on an aqueduct itself, repair of the damage would be geometrically slower than simply repairing a canal berm.

Just such an attack took place the night of 12/13 August 1940. Five RAF Hampdens found the Ems aqueducts in bright moonlight and got one hit with a delayed action bomb.[2] The single hit on the older, weaker aqueduct, halted traffic on the Dortmund-Ems Canal for ten days. Those ten days were important since they represented delays in the German build-up of barges and equipment for the invasion of England.

To help protect against a repeat attack, the aqueduct was partially camouflaged (photo 5-25). A short section of the Ems River had been covered with cloth panels. The camouflage was carefully sloped from the aqueduct down to the panels covering the river to insure that the aqueduct shadow did not give the site away. Though the camera let a photo interpreter look right through the netting, it would have been reasonably effective in hiding the river from a low flying bomber at night. One of the most significant contributions of this netting was to kill off the reflection of

2. Flight Lieutenant R.A.B. Learoyd, who led the flight and got the hit, was awarded a Victoria Cross for this attack.

moonlight on the river. Under the right conditions and seen from the right angle, reflected moonlight could make a river visible for many miles to a night bomber (which was when the RAF tended to attack).[3]

Bomb damage had stripped back the Ems River netting to show how it was constructed. Damage to the old aqueduct was by-passed by a temporary cofferdam wall that was cross-braced to hold it firm while repairs were made. The temporary wall was necessary to permit water to be introduced in the canal again since there was always a risk of bomb damage to the other aqueduct.

After a year the old aqueduct still showed its bomb damage, but the temporary retaining wall had been fixed to permit water and barges to flow in case the main aqueduct was blown (photo 5-26). Ground scars showed where a pair of deceptions were built to simulate canal traffic at night to draw bombs from the real targets. The Ems River netting had been restored between the aqueducts, but was not yet extensive enough to really hide the river.

The Dortmund-Ems Canal was not attacked again until 15 September 1943, when the target was the canal bank rather than one of the aqueducts.[4] This raid was a failure with heavy losses dissuading the RAF from another attack until 23 September 1944.[5] By that time the old aqueduct had been repaired. Ems River netting had been extended on both sides of the aqueducts (photo 5-27). This made it more difficult for a night bomber to find the critical intersection of canal and river. The netting was still not extended far enough from the canal to really disguise the location of the aqueducts.

An enlargement of photo 5-27 shows a darkening of the narrower canal route (photo 5-28). Since the canal bank was not obscured, the canal darkening may have been paint on the concrete canal flooring. The intent of this darkening would be to make the smaller canal route 'disappear'. The whole effect was to make the aqueduct appear to be just another section of canal rather than a choke-point, and to disguise the characteristic dual aqueduct crossing of the Ems. Part of the effectiveness of the expanded camouflage was negated by a considerable increase

5-17 Hamburg's Dammtor Railway Station in late 1941, before camouflage began.

5-18 The Dammtor station caught in the process of camouflage during the winter of 1941-42 and following spring. From a British Intelligence report.

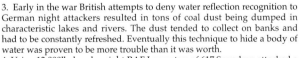

5-19 The Dammtor Station camouflage project was complete when sloping painted material was draped on the north (bottom) side of the structure.

3. Early in the war British attempts to deny water reflection recognition to German night attackers resulted in tons of coal dust being dumped in characteristic lakes and rivers. The dust tended to collect on banks and had to be constantly refreshed. Eventually this technique to hide a body of water was proven to be more trouble than it was worth.

4 Using 12,000lb. bombs, eight RAF Lancasters of 617 Squadron attacked a section of the canal bank at an altitude of 150ft in an attempt to repeat their famous 'Dam Buster' raid. Five planes were lost, including the leader, Squadron Leader Holden, who was piloting the aircraft and crew Guy Gibson had flown to the Mohne Dam. The canal was not breached.

5. On 23 September 1944, while 125 Lancasters went after the canal bank around the Glane River aqueduct at Ladbergen with regular bombs, Wing Commander G.L. Cheshire led eleven 617 Squadron aircraft against the aqueduct again. Bombing from 8,000 feet with 12,000lb bombs, they closed the Dortmund-Ems Canal until 21 October 1944.

5-20 By 18 August 1943 the Hamburg Dammtor Railway Station had changed appearance since photo 5-17. It was still given away by shadows and the characteristic surrounding open areas.

5-21 Disguising a railway yard was no easy trick. The inability to keep up the camouflage at either end gave a yard away. In this example from Stuttgart, Germany, an adjacent factory and canal were also camouflaged, 7 May 1942.

5-22 Stuttgart marshalling yard, industrial and canal camouflage sometime after photo 5-21.

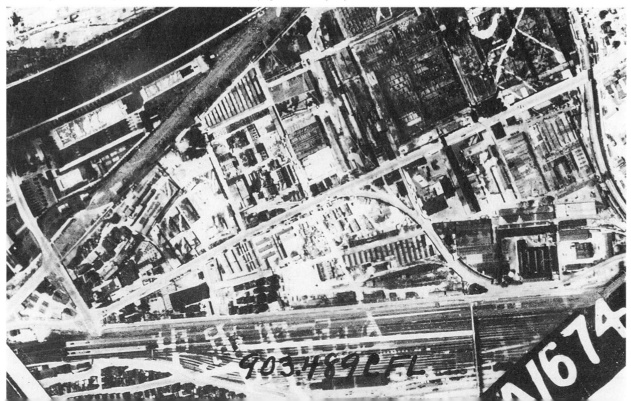

5-23 Canals were particularly vulnerable to air attack since spilling their water at a low point could shut down large sections of the system, and repairs were most difficult. Aqueduct over a rail line, Eberswalde, Germany, pre-war photo.

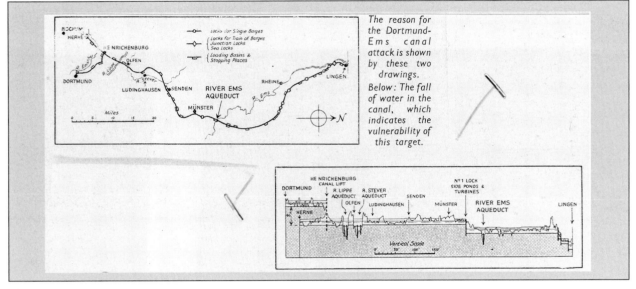

5-24 One of Germany's key transportation targets was the Dortmund-Ems Canal where it passed over the Ems River near Münster.

in track activity (paths and small roads) around the aqueducts.

The Dortmund-Ems Canal remained a target through the war, but the aqueducts were deemed too costly to hit until absolute control of the air was attained. After the fall of 1944 the canal was hit regularly and eventually crippled.[6] The aqueduct camouflage was still up when US heavy bombers attacked in the area in March 1945 (photo 5-29). A profusion of new bomb craters and the obvious ease of seeing the target proved the Ems River netting was an anachronism by that date.[7]

The Kleine Weser River at Bremen was not only a waterway, it was a conspicuous landmark (annotation A) as was the City Water Works (annotation B), leading Allied bombers to targets all over the city (photo 5-30). The first photograph in this series shows the beginnings of framework grids that would cover the river and Water Works (annotation C).

In the second reconnaissance photo, the framework had progressed to nearly cover a section of river (photo 5-31). Pilings were driven into the river to support a wooden grid that, in turn, was covered with material. Painting had begun on the material to make it blend into the surrounding ground (annotation A). The Water Works got the

---

6. The canal was hit with 930 tons of bombs during the night of 4/5 November 1944, redamaging the Ems River aqueduct. Just as the repaired canal was about to open it was bombed again at both Ladbergen and Gravenhorst the night of 21/22 November, closing it until 10 December 1944. Bombed again on 1 January 1945, the canal did not reopen until 6 February and was not navigable past Gravenhorst for the rest of the war. A 7 February bombing closed the canal until 16 February. It was hit again five days later and on 21 February and 3 March. Navigation never reopened beyond Ladbergen after these attacks.

7. The 21 March 1945 attack was not on the canal but was part of a massive bombing of the Rühr and vicinity as preparation for the Allied crossing of the lower Rhine on 23 March.

134

same camouflage attention with its open aeration pools covered with curved, darkened structures (annotation B).

When nearly complete, the extensive Kleine Weser camouflage project covered a large stretch of the river and very effectively hid the Water Works (photo 5-32). The only part of the river that showed was a small section left open to permit boat access to the jetties (annotation A). Camouflage over different parts of the Water Works had been joined together to make a scene totally different than the original. If British Intelligence had not been watching the entire process with aerial reconnaissance, this camouflage might have been quite effective.

Typical of the problems of large-area camouflage projects, the Water Works structure was more difficult to maintain over time than to construct. During the winter of 1941-42, before the Kleine Weser River camouflage was completed, nature defeated the project (photo 5-33). Movement of ice in the river uprooted pilings and snow weighed down the painted covering. The camouflage collapsed over a large area in the centre (annotation A). The less ambitious and more effective camouflage of the Water Works survived the elements but lost most of its value as the overall camouflage context was damaged. Also, the dark summer and fall colours on the Water Works stood out starkly against the white winter landscape.

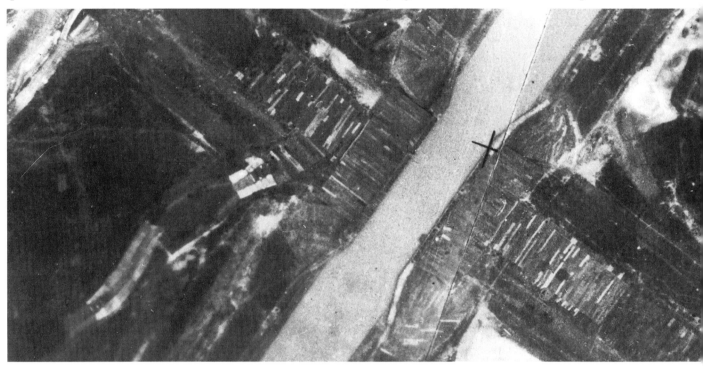

5-25 Enlargement of imagery from the fall of 1940 showed improvement in the camouflage nets over the Ems and repair work on the old aqueduct bomb damage.

5-26 Photography of 18 August 1941 showed bomb damage to the old aqueduct unrepaired a year after it was hit by the RAF. Barges were active on the new aqueduct.

Text within image: New Aqueduct A · Part of dummy canal · River Ems camouflaged · Old Aqueduct B · 6(b) 5.a/6 · DORTMUND · EMS CANAL · Aqueducts over Ems North of Münster · 500 · 1000 Yards

5-27 *British target graphic of the Dortmund-Ems Canal aqueducts over the Ems, showing camouflage and decoy work.*

5-28 *Enlargement of photo 5-27 showing detail of the camouflage nets over the Ems.*

Text within image: r Ems · mouflaged · Old Aqueduc

5-29 Dortmund-Ems Canal aqueducts over the Ems as they appeared on 21 March 1945. Camouflage still covered the Ems but new craters prove that Allied bombers could find this target. The falling bombs (arrows) were not aimed at the canal.

5-30 British photoreconnaissance documented the start of German attempts to camouflage key bomb-aiming landmarks in Bremen in the summer of 1941.

5-31 *Throughout the summer of 1941 the Kleine Weser River and Bremen City Water Works were gradually covered with a framework and canopy of material for camouflage.*

5-32 *The Kleine Weser River camouflage project at Bremen was nearly completed by the fall of 1941.*

5-33 *Snow and river ice during the 1941-42 winter caused part of the Bremen Kleine Weser River camouflage to collapse.*

CHAPTER 6

HIDING THE HEART

Camouflaging Industrial Targets

Industrial targets were the most lucrative and most vulnerable objectives of bomber activity and all the warring nations quite rightly expected their industrial base to receive a lot of attention from enemy planes.

Large industrial complexes were sitting ducks. To make matters worse, the locations of most of major industries were well known before the war, and none of the buildings had been designed with bomb damage, much less camouflage, in mind.[1] Further, major industrial plants, or those making some unique part, were hard for a nation to replace. Their specialised equipment, facilities, distribution systems and trained labour pools were mutually interdependent. Interruption of any of these aspects of production created a condition that could undermine an entire industry, and that had a direct impact on the war effort of any nation.

To make matters worse for those on the ground, industries were usually easy for intelligence to locate and watch from the air (photo 6-1). Even when surrounded by urban development, industries were relatively simple to find on aerial photography (photo 6-2). For a bomb-aimer five miles overhead, with only a few seconds to pick out an aiming point through smoke, searchlight glare at night, and flak, finding an industrial complex was not so easy –but certainly not impossible. It was the slim chance of saving even part of an industrial complex that resulted in considerable resources being applied to active and passive defences.

Key installations or complexes were so important they were ringed with anti-aircraft artillery and had fighter planes positioned to block on-coming bombers. Even with active defences protecting them, the loss of a major industry was a price so high that many plants also resorted to all manner of camouflage as a passive defence in spite of the twin disadvantages of known locations and large areas to disguise.[2]

In all the warring nations, initial attempts at factory camouflage were local initiatives, usually from the efforts of a diligent plant manager trying to protect his resources. Their fanciful ideas of what would hide their factory from airmen were often counterproductive, actually calling attention to the place, even from high altitude. Apparently in the first days of war it was 'intuitively obvious' that any pattern daubing of paint involving two or more colours counted as camouflage.

Paint

The two industrial camouflage paint jobs most frequently encountered in the war were dazzle and random disruptive patterns. Dazzle patterns might have worked at sea, but were hopeless on the land.[3] Rather than disguise a factory, dazzle camouflage tended to make it more conspicuous (photo 6-3). In fact, early in the war, bomb-aimers were sometimes able to locate key aiming points by their camouflage (photo 6-4). On the land, dazzle patterns violated the basic commandment of camouflage – they did not blend into the background. To make matters worse, dazzle did not even break up shadows to deny enemy photo intelligence that most valuable tool in understanding what was happening on the ground. Surprisingly, some of the dazzle camouflage jobs were carefully touched up and maintained well into the war in spite of their lack of effectiveness.[4]

The second time-honoured and generally ineffective paint camouflage for industry was a random disruptive pattern. At best these patterns tended to break up the straight lines of a factory complex. More often they drew attention to the buildings (photo 6-5). Typically, early random pattern camouflage work was just done on the main factory buildings themselves. Failure to consider the surroundings, such as parking lots, roads and rail lines usually negated any small advantage of camouflage based upon painted roofs alone.

---

1. Of course this did not apply to factories dealing with hazardous or explosive materials which were carefully designed to confine damage from accidental fires or explosions. Many conventional industrial buildings also had internal fire walls, but these were totally inadequate against bomb damage.

2. Major factory locations were all well known (except in Japan and, to a lesser extent, the Soviet Union). The United Kingdom, United States, and German Europe were pretty much an open book based upon pre-war information. Only factories constructed after the war began were unknown and then only if enemy intelligence collection capabilities could not reach them.

3. As a guess, dazzle camouflage on factories probably came from local factory management remembering photos of WW I ships which were frequently done in this camouflage style.

4. After 1942, it was the Allies who were doing the increasingly deep penetration bombing of industrial targets. Dazzle paintwork was often used on small factories in Nazi occupied Europe that did not rise to a point of interest on Allied target lists until 1943–44. Local authorities apparently misunderstood this lack of target importance as a testimonial to their camouflage style.

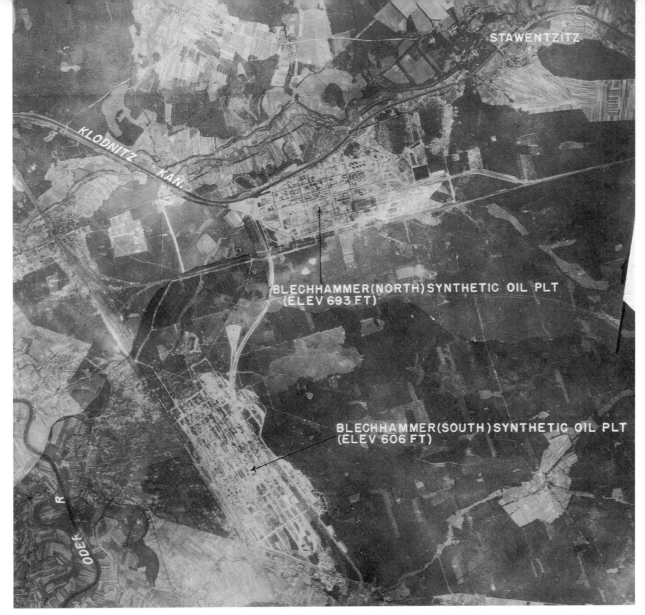

6-1 Even on small-scale photography, isolated industries stood out like a blot on the landscape. These are the giant Blechhammer synthetic oil plants, 60 miles south-east of Breslau, Germany (now Wroclaw, Poland). US target graphic using imagery of 15 August 1944.

When a random pattern paint job was combined with extension of the camouflage to the surrounding ground, the effect was improved (photo 6-6). The big problem with this type of 'paint only' camouflage was that it did not cover shadows or transportation arteries that could identify the complex. Painted random pattern camouflage that spread beyond the buildings themselves was moderately effective against night bombing.

The next step forward in industrial camouflage sophistication was the use of paint patterns designed specifically to blend the key buildings into their background. Superficially these were random patterns, but in reality they were thoughtfully guided by the overall setting. Since most factory complexes were in an urban setting, the more successful camouflage paint patterns had to make factory buildings look like houses or inconsequential commercial structures.

Determined attempts to make it hard to aim a bomb at a major factory required imagination, skill and a favourable surrounding. At Hannover in Germany the Continental Gummiwerke (rubber products factory) was painted to look like the surrounding buildings and streets (photo 6-7). A lack of shadows from the painted buildings and the

ease of seeing approaching spur tracks made this camouflage unconvincing.

When viewed in its overall context the Hannover factory camouflage appeared even more obvious (photo 6-8). The painted buildings were too light and unaltered open spaces were a tip-off to intelligence analysts.[5] A similar crude paint camouflage was used on the railway station just up the line with the same unconvincing results. Once again, if the surrounding areas were not part of the camouflage, paint on a factory roof did not work (photo 6-9). Conversely, when done carefully and completely throughout a factory complex the effect could be quite good (photo 6-10). Shadows and roads were still a problem but at night neither of these would help a bomb-aimer. Even in daylight and seen on an enlarged aerial photograph, a thoroughly done painted urban pattern was moderately effective when it closely matched the neighbouring buildings (photo 6-11).

---

5. The strong white line surrounding the Gummiwerke buildings on one side of the tracks is a WW II target annotation and not part of the camouflage or the image. This factory was the largest of its type in Germany, producing 90% of the aircraft tyres and 50% of the tank and truck tyres.

140

6-2 *Industries merged into an urban pattern were harder to find—but not too hard. Schweinfurt, Germany, 24 July 1944. Arrows show key war industries (clockwise from 12 o'clock): Kugelfischer ball-bearing plant, V.K.F. Deutsche Gusstahlkugel und Maschinenfabrik A.G. Werke I, Ultra Marine factory, V.K.F Werke II, Deutsche Star ball-bearing plant, Fechtel und Sachs A.G.*

6-3 *Early World War II 'dazzle' style disruptive paint job on a small factory in Germany.*

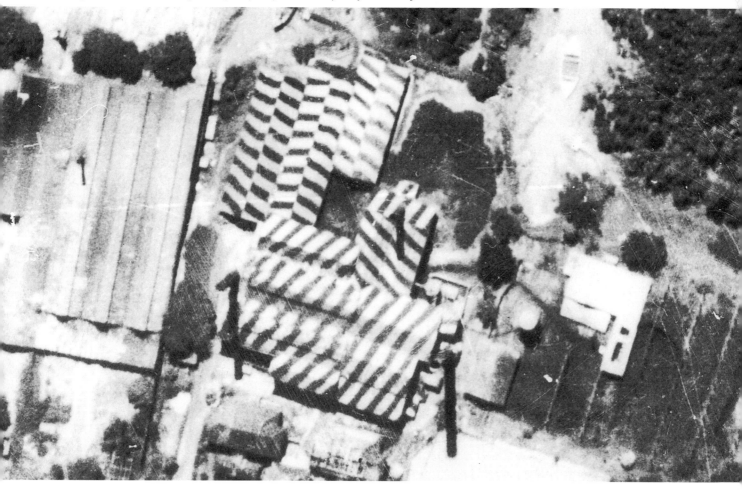

6-4 Camouflage paint schemes on a German defence industry hid little. It probably actually called attention to the building. British photography, 19 August 1943.

6-5 US photo of the Republic Aviation factory, Long Island, New York, 6 May 1942. The sharp building outline and shadow and the parking areas gave this camouflage away.

6-6 German photo of a British munitions plant painted to break up building outlines, 4 December 1940.

6-7 A major industry was easily given away by the associated railway tracks. The Continental Gummiwerke plant was painted to look like the surrounding apartments and streets. Hannover, Germany, 6 July 1941.

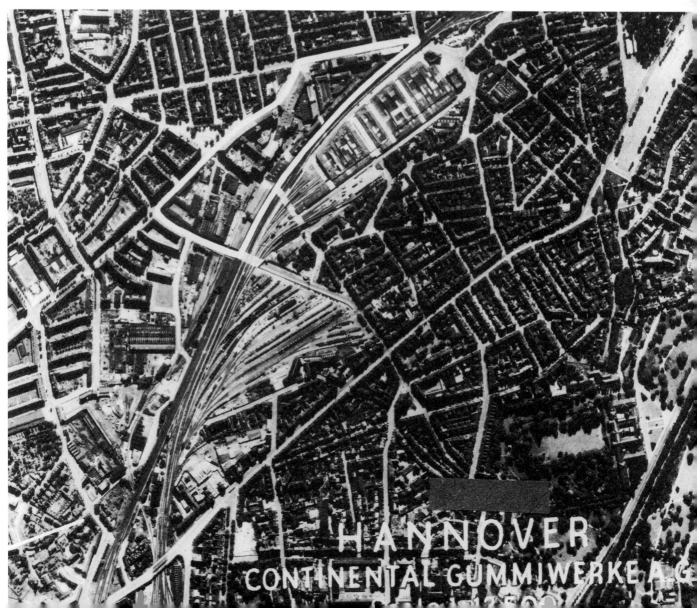

HANNOVER
CONTINENTAL GUMMIWERKE A.G

6-8 Painted camouflage of the Continental Gummiwerke in its overall context, Hannover, Germany, 6 July 1941. The railway station at upper right was also camouflaged with simple paintwork.

6-9 Enlargement of a camouflaged Japanese factory not well tied into its background. South-west of Tokyo, 30 August 1945.

Occasionally the configuration of the buildings to be disguised and the surrounding pattern to be copied, presented a problem so complex that no art or effort could solve it with paint alone. An example of this occurred at Alexandria in Egypt where the British tried to hide huge dock warehouses as small native houses (photo 6-12). This type of camouflage worked much better on smaller structures such as oil storage tanks (some of which are indicated on the photo by arrows).

Oil tanks and refineries were a special class of target. They were thin skinned and densely sited, making them vulnerable to blast, fire and fragment damage. What the tanks and refineries contained was valuable but replacing the oil or gas was easier than replacing the refining capability or the storage tanks positioned to keep the petroleum products in handy locations. Finally, damaged petroleum lines or storage tanks usually leaked and caught fire, spreading the damage and creating an aiming point for subsequent bombers. For these reasons enemy petroleum targets got special treatment from airmen, so they also got special camouflage treatment all over the world.

The most difficult aspect of disguising an oil tank was its round shape. Random pattern painting did

little to alter or disguise either the characteristic outline or shadow (photo 6-13). Simple random patterns were as ineffective from overhead as from a lower angle (photo 6-14). Some tanks got very effective localised camouflage, including minor construction to alter their round appearance. At Pearl Harbor, the US Navy tried a variety of designs to hide the huge oil storage tanks serving the Fleet (photo 6-15). One of the best attempts made one of the tanks look like a small office building (photo 6-16). Failure to camouflage adjacent tanks negated the fine effort on the one tank.[6]

Even more elaborate construction was often effective camouflage. The best were those that completely covered the tanks, making them indistinguishable from surrounding buildings (photo 6-17). Of course, to be effective this type of camouflage had to support making an entire complex harder to find.

Other construction associated with fuel tanks had nothing to do with camouflage. These were dams or walls designed to contain spills. In widely spaced

6. Note the excellent random pattern paint camouflage on the large low building up and to the right on photo 6-16 (compare with photo 6-15).

TARGET 1544
NEW OTA PLANT
NAKAJIMA AIRCRAFT COMPANY
INDUSTRIAL REPORT NO.3
C.I.U. XXI BOM. COM.
R/F_1/9700
PHOTOGRAPHY OF 7 NOV1944
NO.789
N

6-10 XXI Bomber Command photo of a Japanese aircraft plant, 7 November 1944.

tanks they took the form of a low earth dike (as on photos 6-15 and 6-16). Closely spaced tanks often had walls around them that were themselves sometimes camouflaged (photo 6-18).

Nets

With large areas to cover, netting was a natural choice for industrial camouflage. Nets were cheap and simple to set up by unskilled labour. They could mask a facility as well as the raw materials, containers and out-put of finished products intelligence needed to see to assess the type, volume and potential of work going on at a factory. Nets were also effective because they did not require modification of the object to be hidden. This means of camouflage was often selected when it was critical to disguise a characteristic shape, such as for oil tanks. To be effective, the netting had to kill the shadow of the tank and blend the shape into the ground. It helped if the tank itself was already partly buried. When done correctly and with sufficient area given camouflage treatment, netting could be very good (photo 6-19). The small oil storage tanks in this example had covering nets with irregular surfaces that completely hid their cylindrical shape.[7] The flaw in this elaborate camouflage was retention of the encircling roads. The road pattern called attention to an area that might otherwise have been by-passed by roving airmen. Further damage was done by the roads because their shape suggested the shape of the objects concealed.[8] Low oblique imagery of the tank farm in photo 6-19 discloses how the nets were positioned (photo 6-20).

A large tank farm in an urban setting presented a more difficult camouflage problem than the small rural installation of photo 6-19. Oil storage tanks at Bremen were a good example (photo 6-21). Circled by spill dikes and blast walls, these tanks were highly visible, their shadows stark and obvious.

One year later the Bremen tank farm was under a blanket of nets (photo 6-22). The camouflage netting was well done, sloping to the ground in most cases and blanking shadows.[9] Attacking airmen would probably have had a hard time seeing these tanks – as you see, a photo interpreter did not. Since the ship channel and curving railway lines bounding

---

7. In fact once you know they are there you can make out the circular shape of the top of the tank on all but one of the camouflage jobs, but then we know where to look and what to look for.

8. The near tank was just a base on photo 6-19. Photo 6-20 shows it under construction after the Allies took the area.

9. Note that alongside the ship channel and at its end, netting covered new tanks built since photo 6-21.

6-11 Enlargement of photo 6-10 to show a camouflage pattern similar to the adjacent village.

6-12 German photography of camouflaged British port facilities and oil storage at Alexandria, Egypt, 24 April 1941.

6-13 Close-in oblique of camouflaged fuel storage tanks at Genoa Fuel, 19 July 1945.

the installation were not camouflaged, the tank farm was thoroughly bombed in spite of its nets (photo 6-23).

Synthetic rubber manufacture was another class of chemical industry on the continent that got priority attention from both Allied bombers and German camoufleurs.[10] An example of this type of plant occurred at Huls, near Dortmund, Germany.[11] The complex structure of pipes, towers and buildings was served by thirty miles of rail spurs that curved into the site like a row of sign posts pointing to the installation.[12] Following attacks early in the war, the Huls plant was camouflaged by one of the most elaborate efforts undertaken anywhere in the Rühr.[13]

At Huls, wire nets heavily garnished with bits of glass wool and cloth were strung over a large area of the plant. This netting was augmented with bunches of cloth, wood and wire, simulating bushes. The entire assembly was repainted periodically to match the changing colours of different seasons.[14] All of this was built at a cost of RM 4 million and required a crew of 25 men full-time to maintain the camouflage.[15]

For some reason the entire factory was not covered, but camouflage nets were draped over the most critical parts of the installation (photo 6-24). Viewed from near ground level the effect appeared

10. Denied a source of rubber by naval blockade, Nazi Germany depended on Buna-S synthetic rubber made in plants at Huls, Ludwigshafen-Oppau, Schkopau, Auschwitz in Poland (after May 1944), and Leverkusen (never in full operation).

11. The Huls synthetic rubber factory was built in 1938. By 1944 it employed 5,500 Germans and 4,500 slave-labourers from Nazi occupied countries. During peak production (March 1944) the Huls works turned out 4,097 tons of rubber per month.

12. The Huls factory occupied about 60 acres of a 541 acre site and was built at a cost of RM 400 million by I.G. Farbenindustrie. Huls was the second largest Buna-S synthetic rubber plant in the Reich, making about a third of the rubber produced. The plant used coal as its raw material and also made glycerine for the explosives industry and glycol for engine coolant as by-products of the synthetic rubber process.

13. The Huls synthetic rubber plant was first attacked the night of 17/18 June 1940 and again on 15/16 August. The RAF did not strike again until 12/13 June, and 6/7 and 12/13 September 1941. The plant did not suffer real damage until an RAF raid on 28/29 December 1941. It took three months to get back to full production. The factory did not get hit hard again until a 182-plane raid by the US Eighth Air Force on 22 June 43 that took six months of rebuilding to overcome. Huls was attacked by small or abortive air raids five more times during the rest of the war, but none had a major impact on plant production.

14. The Huls camouflage was extremely unpopular with the workers. They still got bombed, sections rusted and collapsed without warning, blew down in strong winds and the paint and dyes dripped onto their clothes as they walked beneath. In addition, the netting hindered air circulation and made it more difficult to fight fires.

15. Huls also had its own smoke generation capability and a major decoy plant located four miles to the east. The decoy – built after the raid of 28 December 1941 – was very realistic from the ground. Lights, decoy fires and explosions were controlled electrically from a central concrete bomb shelter. From the air the decoy was ineffective and not a single bomb went on the decoy during the entire war.

6-14 *A vertical of the camouflaged fuel storage tanks at Genoa, 21 December 1942.*

6-15 *Paint camouflaged fuel storage tanks at Pearl Harbor, 26 November 1941.*

very good (photo 6-25). All this effort must have made an excellent impression on visiting dignitaries. However, viewed from overhead the effect was far less impressive (photo 6-26). Not only were the nets penetrated by the aerial camera (when the prints were viewed in stereo), the surrounding tip-off features were not masked (photo 6-27). The incomplete camouflage of the Huls factory did not stop bombers, but it did make it more difficult for Allied intelligence to assess damage in some parts of the installation following a raid.[16]

Another type of obscuring camouflage extensively employed on factories was the use of garnished or painted strips of cloth mesh (photo 6-28). In this kind of camouflage narrow strips of green and brown coloured material were sewn on rolls of material like fishnet. Long panels of netting were easily rolled up for shipping and were just as easy to install. They could be draped, hung vertically or horizontally, and required little in the way of framework. When augmented by heavier camouflage, such as wrappings of coloured canvas, strip netting was particularly good at killing tell-tale shadows. This style of camouflage was particularly effective in a rural environment, like a dense pine forest. A good example of garnished strip netting was the V-1 assembly plant near

---

16. Because of the hazardous nature of many of the chemicals and processes involved, the Huls plant was laid out as a series of parallel production lines to minimise damage from fires or accidents. It also meant that one of the parallel lines could be knocked out and production maintained. This tended to make overall production at Huls immune to all but the heaviest and most accurate bombing attack.

Dannenberg in Germany. A three-square-mile area of forest, containing 85 buildings, was laced with strip nets. Even though the nets were everywhere they did not cover the installation. They made the site harder to see but did not hide it.

Most industrial sites did not get camouflage as thorough or widespread as the Dannenberg plant. Incomplete area camouflage of sites using nets was more the norm than the exception. A factory near Albert in France was typical (photo 6-29). At this factory, large areas of the complex were netted over and nets ran from roof level to the ground in several places. A portion of the incoming rail line was covered over. A few damning shadows and the curving railway spur were the keys to finding this factory. Both of these camouflage flaws would have been easy to eliminate, certainly easy after the effort expended in the rest of the complex.

The final type of netting was a blanket cover to completely mask a target. Two miles south-east of Albert, near the village of Meaulte, was one of the best examples of blanket netting in Nazi Europe. The prospective target was the Potez Aircraft factory which was being used by the Luftwaffe to repair fighter planes (photo 6-30). The large aircraft assembly buildings overshadowed the airfield buildings just across the road. When the RAF started actively bombing Nazi war production assets in 1941, the Potez factory was camouflaged by a complete covering of netting and cloth painted to look like the surrounding field pattern (photo 6-31).

The Potez factory was hidden much like the Rocklea munitions plant near Brisbane, Australia. At that site an umbrella of chicken-wire garnished with strips of cloth covered the factory (photo 6-32). Camouflage extended well beyond roof eaves, sloping towards the ground to disrupt shadows and mask the buildings from a low angle view. Underneath the netting the buildings were painted in random disruptive patterns and allowed to stick through the camouflage where necessary for light and ventilation. Fake trees, bushes and roads adorned factory roofs (photo 6-33). The entire effort was well designed to break up the lines and

shadows of factory buildings. Nothing was done to disguise telephone poles or smokestacks (probably because of the fire hazard).

At Meaulte, a tall tower in the factory stuck up through the netting disguised as a small house. No shadows showed, no roads entered the area. To a bomber overhead the factory was invisible. To a photo interpreter the faint outlines of some of the buildings were still discernible, but the heavy netting and constructions effectively denied Intelligence any information on factory production. This camouflage was good.

Of course, the airfield buildings were still obvious, and British Intelligence knew that the factory was just over the road. When photo 6-31 was taken, the Potez factory had been bombed on the previous day 28 August 1942, (see photo 6-34) by the US Eighth Air Force, and the camouflage had apparently worked. Bomb damage to structures was annotated on the photo by RAF intelligence technicians. The attack seems to have concentrated on the airfield, although the aircraft factory was the target. Just two bomb craters show in the factory area and both have the look of strays.

Decoys

The Potez factory at Meaulte was close enough to England to receive considerable attention from the RAF and it was therefore given an added passive defence.[17] A decoy factory and airfield combination was built two miles further to the south-east of Meaulte (photo 6-34). The decoy buildings were about the right size but they were remote from any villages and situated in open fields with no roads and showing no traces of activity. The fake installation should have been easy to identify and ignore but 'green' US aircrews fell for the decoy on 28 August 1942.[18] The mistake was embarrassing to the new Eighth Air Force, but understandable. The

---

17. Meaulte was just 140 miles from bomber bases in East Anglia and barely 100 miles from Allied fighter bases in Kent.

18. Photo 6-32 shows at least 20 bombs that missed the decoy target.

6-16 Oblique view of camouflage in the Pearl Harbor tank farm, 24 October 1943.

6-17 *A small, well-camouflaged oil refinery near Düsseldorf, Germany, 9 November 1941.*

6-18 *Disruptive paint on blast walls around oil tanks, Ploesti, Romania, 1 August 1943.*

6-19 Vertical enlargement of a small tank farm in Burma, 1944. The photo shows the paths that gave this fine camouflage away.

6-20 Oblique view of net camouflaged fuel tanks. Burma, 1944.

6-21 Oil tanks at Bremen's Deutsche Vacuum Refinery had disruptive paint and blast walls but were otherwise exposed, 1941.

6-22 The oil storage tanks in photo 6-21 after camouflage. Nets were erected to kill shadows. The camera saw right through the nets but an aircrew would not have been able to see the tanks.

camouflage was very well executed and the decoy was fairly convincing. It was only the sixth attack by the Eighth, and some of the crews were on their first combat mission.[19] Nets were not to save the Potez factory for long.[20]

By 1943 it was clear to Nazi administrators that camouflage, no matter how good, was not enough in the face of the growing Allied bomber offensive. Decoys had been used for key installations since 1941, but two years later they sprang up around nearly every major factory. The more important the industry, then the more elaborate the decoy. Some were quite good.

Occasionally, a single group of decoy buildings could serve more than one target. Just such a decoy complex existed at Puchheim in Germany, about four miles north-west of a pair of heavy industrial targets at Munich (photo 6-35). At Allach there was the Junkers aircraft engine factory and nearby the Krauss steam locomotive works (photo 6-36).[21] To aid the deception, the Junkers plant was camouflaged, but the effort was crude. A disruptive

random pattern and painted road hardly overrode the vista of a sprawling industrial complex with sharp building shadows and large ground scars from new construction (photo 6-37). Interestingly enough, parts of the plant were netted over. Painted nets slanted from below roof level to the ground on the buildings with painted roofs. A group of five small administrative or laboratory buildings was covered by a sheer, plain net but the characteristic engine test cells with their square roof vents were left undisguised.

Decoy installations figured heavily in the defence of the German synthetic fuels industry. One of the main plants was Politz in Pomerania near Stettin (now Szczecin, Poland). The Politz facility was so deep in Nazi Europe that it was beyond Allied bomber range until 1943. However, the plant was watched by Allied intelligence as it was built and went into operation (photo 6-38).

As early as October 1941, RAF photoreconnaissance had discovered a decoy Politz a few miles from the real plant (photo 6-39). This elaborate decoy was the right shape, displayed a number of buildings, roads, lights and had provision for fires to simulate damage. In daylight the decoy appeared crude – the open fields, lack of activity and absence of incoming roads would not fool anyone. At night this decoy was good.

In case the principal decoy did not work or airmen took an approach that did not take them near the decoy, several other decoys were constructed (photo 6-40). One of the alternate decoys featured dummy oil tanks, a fake wharf and

---

19. The first US heavy bomber attack on the continent from England occurred on 17 August at Rouen in France. Eighth Air Force B-17s had been back over Europe just four times before eleven bombers went to Meaulte on 28 August.

20. The Eighth Air Force went back to Meaulte with 30 B-17s on 6 September, and lost two – the first US heavies lost out of England. Another 30 planes attacked the Potez factory on 2 October 1942.

21. The Krauss works were making light tanks and armoured cars by 1942.

6-23 *Proof that the camouflage in photo 6-22 did not work. Netting can be seen at upper right and at the end of the ship channel. Bremen, 9 July 1945. (DAVA-USArmy)*

6-24 *I.G. Farben synthetic rubber plant near Huls, Germany, camouflaged with well garnished wire netting. Photographed after the war. (DAVA-USArmy)*

6-25 The Huls synthetic rubber plant seen in a view opposite to photo 6-24. Garnished netting, dotted with clumps of cloth simulating bushes, covered a large section of this key German industrial complex. (DAVA-USArmy)

6-26 The Huls synthetic rubber plant on a 3x enlargement of an aerial photograph taken on 15 July 1945. The camouflage that looked so good from the ground did little when viewed from above.

6-27 The 15 July 1945 photo of Huls viewed at its original scale. Despite a considerable camouflage effort the factory was easy to find.

6-28 A V-1 assembly plant near Dannenberg, Germany, camouflaged with bands of cloth mesh striped with coloured cloth. This netting was hung horizontally and vertically through a three square mile area of dense pine forest containing 85 buildings, April 1945. (DAVA-USArmy)

RESTRICTED

6-29 Nets used at a Nazi war industry near Albert, Belgium, 1 December 1943. It is hard to understand what the camoufleurs thought was being achieved by this casual use of camouflage.

a dummy pipeline. This decoy was placed in open fields, 5½ miles from the real plant. Again, the dummy installation would not fool a day bomber but might trick or confuse an aircrew at night. Aerial photos taken a year later showed this decoy falling into disrepair with not a bomb crater to be seen (photo 6-41). Apparently both the Allies and the Nazis had decided that the decoy was not working. The real Politz synthetic fuels plant paid the price for the failure of its defences (photo 6-42).

The Germans went to even greater lengths to protect the Skoda arms factory at Pilsen in Czechoslovakia (photo 6-43). One of the foremost armaments complexes in the world, the Skoda works were turning out tanks and heavy artillery for the Nazi war machine. This group of factories was situated on the outskirts of the hometown of Pilsner beer (photo 6-44). The Skoda complex was easy to find. It had been in the same location since the turn of the century and was certainly no secret. It was also densely packed with hard-to-replace machine shops and foundries. All in all, a dream of a target.

As a concession to the war, or because of age, the factory roofs were blackened and dulled. Across open fields along the city perimeter was a pointer to the Skoda installation. This was the distinctive hub-and-spoke shape of the local prison. The prison could not be left as a road sign to the factory, so the Germans covered it with nets (photos 6-45 and 6-46).

Three miles out in the countryside was one of the largest industrial decoys in the Third Reich (photo 6-47). The Skoda decoy had been thoroughly thought out and showed a lot of attention to detail. The shape of the prison was even duplicated in the right direction and at the right distance from the factory buildings. This decoy was distinguished

by having an unusually large number of decoy buildings, all of which were the correct shape and in the right relative position in the factory group (photo 6-48). There were no roads in the decoy, but fuel tanks, smoke stacks, and Venturi water coolers were faithfully – if skimpily – reproduced (photo 6-49).

Like other early war decoys on the continent, the Skoda deception was designed against RAF night bombing operations. Seemingly accidental lights and the glow of fires in the factory complex, along with blazing lights at the fake prison, were supposed to be convincing to navigators and bomb-aimers. The Skoda decoy worked well at night even though British Intelligence had photographed it by 1942. The decoy was good enough to cause the U.S. 15th Air Force to bomb short of the target on its first daylight bombing trip to Pilsen.[22] They did not make the same error a second time.

Hiding in the Rubble
In late 1944 and early 1945 the Allies had the ability to bomb almost at will, so the Germans came up with a new version of paint, net, and construction camouflage. While new in execution, the concept was just an adaptation of the old rule of blending into the environment. Since the factories and cities were in ruins, the idea was to protect a previously bombed factory by making it look like it was destroyed and abandoned.

Walls were painted to look like rubble (photos 6-50 and 6-51). Nets garnished with pieces of glazed cloth were draped over reconstructed areas to

---

22. The Skoda works were attacked by heavy bombers of the Fifteenth Air Force on 16 and 32 October, and 9, 16 and 20 December 1944. In 1945 the factories were raided on 1, 4, 11, 15, 16, 17, and 18 April.

6-30 The Potez aircraft factory at Meaulte, France, before camouflage.

6-31 After an exceptionally good job of painted net camouflage, the Potez factory was nearly invisible, but not its airfield neighbour.

6-32 Rocklea munitions factory near Brisbane, Australia, September 1943. Chicken wire garnished with strips of cloth extended beyond the roof lines to kill shadows and oblique observation. (DAVA-USArmy)

6-33 Rocklea munitions plant showing garnished wire mesh and a false road going over the roof, September 1943. (DAVA-USArmy)

6-34 A decoy factory was added at Meaulte and it got a share of the bombs on 28 August 1942.

6-35 *Sometimes a decoy served more than one target, as here near Munich.*

6-36 *Junkers aircraft engine plant and Krauss locomotive works at Allach, Germany. Both were served by the decoy in photo 6-35.*

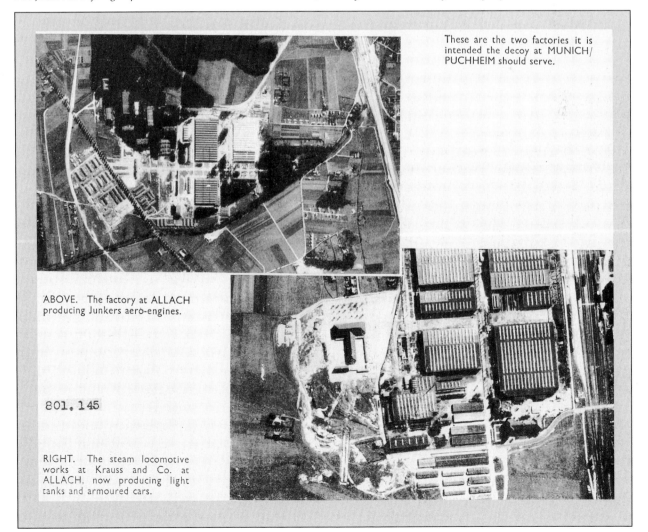

These are the two factories it is intended the decoy at MUNICH/ PUCHHEIM should serve.

ABOVE. The factory at ALLACH producing Junkers aero-engines.

801.145

RIGHT. The steam locomotive works at Krauss and Co. at ALLACH, now producing light tanks and armoured cars.

6.37 *The Junkers aircraft motor plant at Allach, near Munich had been photographed by the British on 18 September 1941 – before it was camouflaged. Painted buildings could not hide the works on 6 September 1943.*

6-38 *Even deep in Germany, key factories used camouflage protection. Politz synthetic oil plant, Pomerania, 22 April 1943.*

6-39 *A decoy for the Politz plant had been photographed by the RAF as early October 1941.*

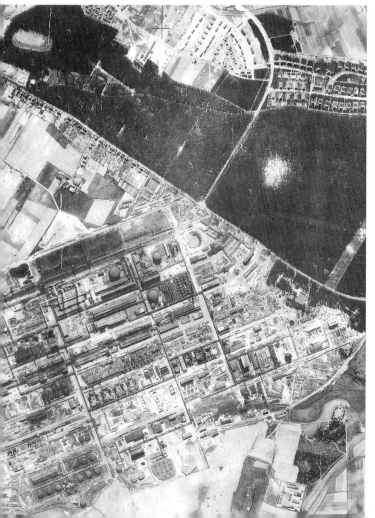

6-40 Another Politz decoy was photographed 17 April 1942.

6-41 The decoy Politz tank farm on 23 June 1943 showed signs of neglect. An absence of bomb craters proves that this decoy fooled no one.

6-42 Destruction and bomb craters in the real Politz synthetic oil plant show that Allied airmen had no problem identifying the real target. RAF photo, 22 March 1945.

6-43 One of the greatest arms factories in the world, the Skoda Works at Pilsen, Czechoslovakia. Photo from 1929.

simulate piles of broken cement or bricks (photo 6-52). Cleverest of all, bombed factories were rebuilt under their blasted roofs (photo 6-53). The new walls were painted aeroplane black and carefully kept inside the shadows of the old ruined walls and roof lines (photo 6-54). Shattered parts of the original factory were intentionally left in place and paths were made with only the minimum essential clearance for plant operation (photo 6-55). Bent girders, piles of broken cement, and twisted sheets of metal were strategically placed over the new factory structures (photo 6-56).

The slightest lapse in camouflage discipline would give the game away. New tracks or cleared areas, finished products not under cover, or any other sign of activity would be spotted by the watching eyes carefully screening reconnaissance imagery. One supposedly destroyed plant had its excellent rebuilt capability negated because a new guard shack was built near the gate.[23] This was hardly appropriate for an abandoned factory and the plant became a target again.

Smoke

By the end of World War II smoke screens were used by hundreds of individual factories as well as entire industrial areas. At the end of the war in Europe smoke was the most common industrial defence. In fact, smoke was probably the first factory defence technique used in World War II (photo 6-57). This type of protection had the disadvantage of calling attention to the area being screened. It also required a good deal of

time to build up to a decent level (photo 6-58). At best, smoke screens interrupted aiming from the air, but did not preclude bombing. Even on a massive scale, such as blanketing a huge area around Berlin, artificial smoke did not stop aerial bombardment, it just made it less precise (photo 6-59).

Out of Sight

Just as an unusual or unexpected location was an excellent adjunct to camouflage, proper positioning was important to a good disguise. The ultimate camouflage was to be in an unusual, remote setting that could not be photographed by enemy intelligence. A good example of this principle was the use of road or rail tunnels or old mines (photo 6-60). Since the entire works were underground tip-offs had to come primarily from agents or enemy radio transmissions. A photo interpreter could only find such an installation through carelessness on the ground. Piles of freshly excavated earth, raw materials or unusual transportation patterns might cause an extra look at an underground installation. Careful examination of a suspect area might disclose a finished aeroplane wing, tank or gun that would expose the nature of the factory activity.

Sometimes there was no tangible evidence, but circumstantial evidence was enough to convince targeteers that something 'fishy' was going on. Photo 6-60 is an example of this type of deduction. Housing for workers at a highway tunnel site would hardly require camouflage. When seemingly normal buildings were observed with camouflage painted roofs the inescapable inference was that the site was more than it seemed to be.

---

23. The Kugelfischer Ball Bearing plant at Ebelsbach in Germany.

6-44 *Pilsen and the Skoda Works from the air. German photo, 9 July 1943.*

6-45 *No attempt was made to hide the sprawling factory complex, but the nearby prison was netted over. German photo, 27 July 1942.*

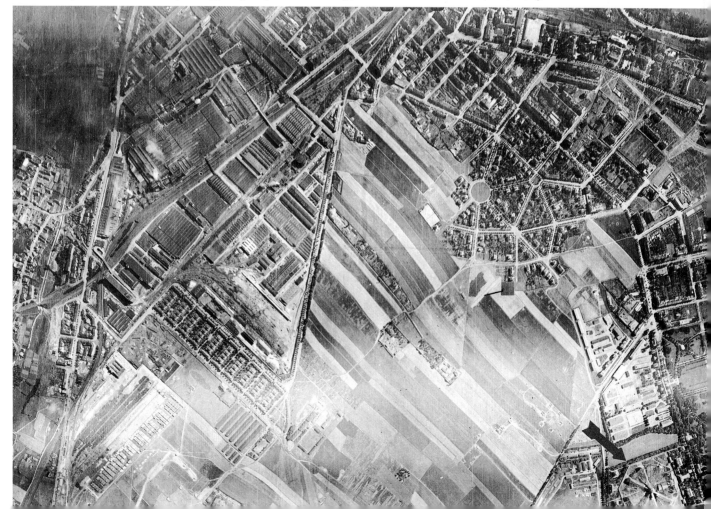

6-46 Post-war photo of the Pilsen prison camouflage.

6-47 A few miles from Pilsen, the Germans erected an elaborate dummy factory and prison. German photo, 24 July, 1942.

6-48 Post-war shot of the dummy Skoda factory.

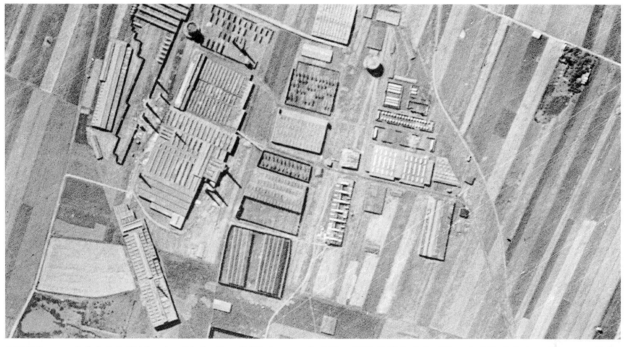

6-49 Enlargement of photo 6-47 (above) matched with a slightly larger scale, 7 May, 1942. British photo of the actual Skoda factory. Compare activity.

6-50 Debris painted on a reconstructed elevator shaft in the Kugelfischer plant at Schweinfurt, Germany. Post-war photo.

6-51 A rebuilt wall in the Schweinfurt Kugelfischer plant painted to look like a damaged wall. Post-war photo.

6-52 Nets garnished with glazed cloth simulate debris over rebuilt areas of the Kugelfischer ball-bearing plant at Ebelsbach, Germany. Post-war photo.

6-53 *Camouflage nets and junk on top of new reinforced concrete construction to simulate debris and destruction. V.K.F. ball-bearing plant, Schweinfurt, Germany. Post-war photo.*

6-54 *Reconstructed walls were painted matte black and kept well inside the shadows of ruined roofs and walls. Kugelfischer plant at Ebelsbach, Germany. Post-war photo.*

6-55 *Oblique view of the Ebelsbach Kugelfischer plant. It appears destroyed; in reality it was still turning out ball-bearings in rooms carefully rebuilt and concealed under the rubble. Post-war photo.*

6.56 *Reconstructed workspaces under rubble at the Ebelsbach Kugelfischer works. Actual debris was artfully placed on top of the new roofs. Post-war photo.*

168

6-57 A primitive way to 'hide' an installation. Byskovice, Poland, autumn of 1939.

6-58 As a German reconnaissance plane circled, the Polish smoke screen quickly covered the installation, calling more attention to it than hiding it.

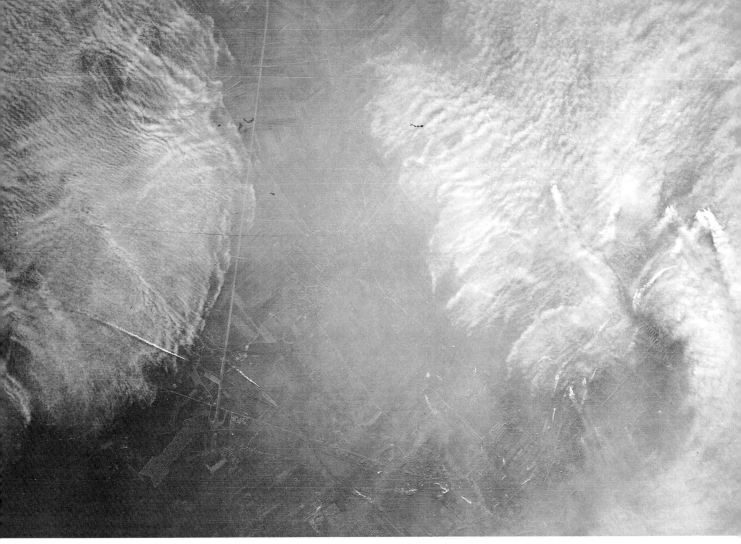

6-59 Smoke screens were far more sophisticated 68 months after photo 6-58 was taken. A huge area north of Berlin was covered by artificial fog on 20 April 1945. A major autobahn intersection was just visible.

6-60 Better than any smoke screen, the ultimate camouflage: a German war industry inside an Autobahn tunnel, Leonberg, 13 May 1944. Materials or end products carelessly left in view might let intelligence locate an installation like this, but not to see or analyse it, nor could bombers do much more than damage the entrances.

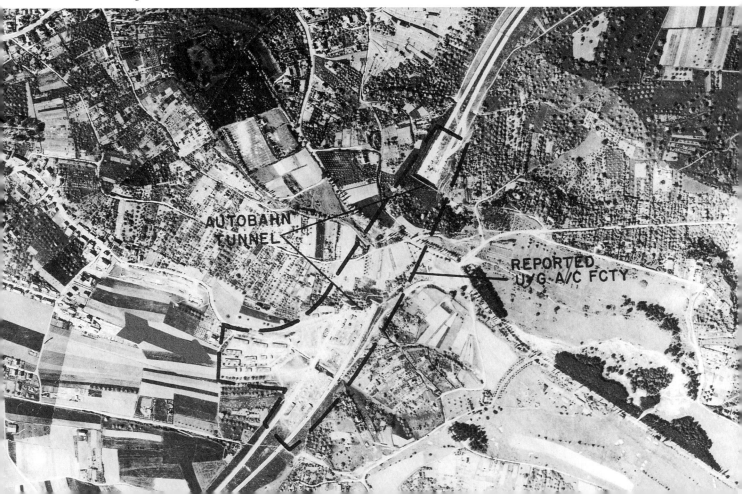

CHAPTER 7

GOOD, BETTER, BEST
Three Case Studies in Large Area Camouflage

An Aircraft Factory

A number of unique circumstances on the West Coast of the United States early in World War II resulted in a showpiece of camouflage that was as useless as it was well done.

In the spring of 1942, Californians were fully expecting to be bombed by the Japanese. The US Fleet was a shambles in Pearl Harbor. Guam, Wake and the Philippines had fallen. American arms had suffered nothing but disasters and there seemed to be no way to halt any new initiative the Japanese cared to make.

Japanese submarines sank a few freighters off Southern Californian ports and shelled oil storage tanks from the Santa Barbara Channel.[1] Planes launched from Japanese submarines had been over US territory in the Pacific Northwest.[2] People on the West Coast were near panic. Southern California was studded with vulnerable targets and critical industries. All those oil refineries, shipyards and aircraft factories were surely high on the enemy's target list. Paranoia over a Japanese attack had even resulted in the 'Battle of Los Angeles' with nervous men firing thousands of rounds of anti-aircraft ammunition into the night sky – at nothing.[3] Many were certain the Japanese carrier fleet that had ravaged Pearl Harbor would reappear to destroy California. Though it seems ludicrous now, landing of invasion troops was not out of the question. People felt helpless to stop anything that might happen. Frustration levels were peaking.

Everybody wanted to do something – anything. Expecting to be in a combat zone at any day, passive protection of the most important installations became a high priority.

A key factor in this story was the special pool of talent available in Hollywood, all eager to help the war effort. Movie studios were full of experts in creating illusion and they had the tools, experience, skills and enthusiasm. They understood how to use wood, wire, cloth, plaster and paint to shape or reshape something. As with most amateur camouflagers, what these people did not have was an understanding of the aerial perspective.

Despite the paranoia, authorities in California were right about one thing: the Japanese had been collecting information on the area for years and knew a great deal about the best targets.[4] One of the most important war assets was the big Douglas Aircraft Company factory at Santa Monica (photo 7-1). Ironically, the plane being produced at the Douglas plant was not a big bomber but the ubiquitous DC-3/C-47, a plane that probably influenced the war as much as any bomber.[5]

A team of personnel from various Hollywood studios working in their own time, took on the job of camouflaging this vital aircraft production plant.[6] Between April and September 1942 this team transformed the Douglas plant to appear as a housing area and created a decoy replica of the plant a few hundred yards away in open fields.

The Douglas factory was butted against urban and light commercial areas along one side and end. The other side and end adjoined unoccupied land. The factory itself was a long line of wide-bay saw-

1. The week before Christmas, 1941, nine Japanese submarines were in US West Coast waters. Submarine *I-10* was off San Diego, *I-19* at Los Angeles and *I-15* off San Francisco. In February 1942 submarine *I-17* ran north from San Diego, firing 13 rounds of 5.5 inch ammunition into the Elewood oil fields north of Santa Barbara on 23 February. She continued on to sink two ships off San Francisco.

2. A biplane from a Japanese submarine made a reconnaissance flight over Seattle on 1 June 1942. On 9 and 29 September the only enemy bombing missions over the United States during WW II were flown by another seaplane from a Japanese submarine. Incendiaries were dropped in the woods of southern Oregon with the intent of starting disastrous forest fires.

3. During the night of 24/25 February 1942, just after the Japanese sub *I-17*'s shelling near Santa Barbara, someone manning an anti-aircraft gun guarding Los Angeles thought he heard a plane and opened fire. All the other gunners around the city thought a battle was on and they just hadn't gotten the word. They opened fire too. No one had a target but before it was over 1,400 rounds of 3-inch ammo and countless smaller calibre rounds had been fired. The 'Battle of Los Angeles' was embarrassing but it also increased the jitters on the West Coast and clearly demonstrates that attacks were expected.

4. Photo 7-1 is a reproduction of a Japanese photo captured when Kiska in the Aleutians was retaken by the US in August 1943. The Japanese caption reads 'The world's greatest bomber in construction at the Douglas Aircraft Company of Santa Monica in California, USA. Four gasoline motors of 2,000 H.P. are appended. Scheduled to be completed this autumn.' 'This autumn' refers to 1941. America was, and still is, a giant security leak; the Japanese probably got this photo from a US magazine before the war.

5. The plane shown under construction was the Douglas XB-19 which was completed in 1941. With a wingspan of 212 feet and an empty weight of 84,431 pounds, this plane was more than twice as big as the B-17, with more than enough range to worry the Japanese. In fact it was just too much plane for its time. The wartime need for rapid mass production of a large number of bombers made the XB-19 prototype a one-of-a-kind.

6. Movie people were some of the first to jump on the 'Victory Program', selling bonds, making training films and entertaining troops as well as helping with camouflage.

7-1 *Reproduction of a Japanese photograph captured on Kiska, in the Aleutians, in August 1943. The Japanese were obviously well aware of the Douglas plant at Santa Monica.*

7-2 *The Douglas Aircraft factory at Santa Monica, California, 28 May 1942. Camouflage of the plant and runway had just begun.*

tooth roofed aircraft assembly buildings and arched-roof hangars (photo 7-2). A wide runway extended the full length of the plant on the side opposite the residential area.

One of the first passive defence measures introduced at the plant was a series of revetted aircraft parking positions on the far side of the runway from the assembly buildings. Next, the entire runway was painted in great rectangles of green, grey and black in preparation for detailed camouflaging. Simultaneously, an area nearly the size of the real plant and runway was graded in the unoccupied land for construction of the decoy.

By August 1942, paint and construction were already making the factory 'disappear' (photo 7-3).

The runway had been converted to a few blocks of urban streets, complete with baseball diamonds, houses and bushes – all two-dimensional and beautifully created. A nice touch was the way the lines of real streets were continued onto the runway with paint. Off to one side, the dummy runway and decoy factory buildings were under construction. Barrage balloons had been added to the factory's passive defences. Circular concrete pads for barrage balloons ringed both the real and bogus installations.

Barrage balloons were over the factory during daylight hours to force enemy bombers to a higher altitude, therefore creating less bombing accuracy. Unfortunately, the cement circles also broke the

172

7-3 Aerial oblique of the Douglas plant, 6 August 1942. Camouflage was well underway. The runway was blended into the local street pattern and most of the buildings were painted. Note the barrage balloons ringing the factory.

camouflage and the balloon pads should also have been toned down.

Meanwhile, the arched roof of a hangar had become a grassy slope dotted with fake houses and bushes (photo 7-4). The details of the scene were remarkable. Houses were made of light plywood with roofs of corrugated sheet metal, but they had windows and fenced yards (photo 7-5). The low trees and bushes were extremely realistic constructions made of 2x4s, chicken wire, and cloth. They would stand up to all but close inspection and they looked very good from a distance (photo 7-6). Actually, they were overkill. An attacking pilot would have already released his bombs well before he got to see the details rendered in this construction.

Still, it was extremely good. Streets and sidewalks were painted on factory roofs or simply panels of white cloth laid on the overall chicken wire framework. 'Cars' parked at the simulated curbs looked ridiculous at close range. From the air the decoy vehicles cast surprisingly realistic shadows and looked like the real thing (photo 7-7). They might even have fooled a Japanese Photo Interpreter, but Japan didn't use aerial photos much for intelligence and had no facility to overfly Santa Monica with a reconnaissance plane.

The fake houses and gentle slopes of simulated grass were carefully positioned to allow factory roof ventilators to function (photo 7-8). Both level-roofed assembly buildings and the arched-roof hangar got the same camouflage treatment. This tended to smooth over differences in height and configuration, blending the entire complex into a cohesive whole. Even the control tower, on top of the hangar, became part of the new landscape.

September saw the actual factory nicely covered by highly effective three-dimensional camouflage. The realism of the two-dimensional camouflage on the runway was outstanding. From roof level, or even looking down from atop the hangar, the effect

was very believable (photo 7-9). Tall poles carrying guy-wires for the camouflage framework did not show from distance or from the air. The sloping of camouflage cover down from roof level tended to kill most of the factory building shadows. Canopies of painted cloth on wire framework covered the aircraft parking area, and made the complex blend into the ground.

When an aerial view was constricted to the plant itself, the effect was still good. Aside from a few unwanted shadows, the only major flaw at this stage of camouflaging was that some of the newly produced aircraft were light-toned (photo 7-10). They stood out conspicuously on seemingly innocent urban streets. Fake factory buildings very nicely duplicated the shape and size relationships of the actual buildings, albeit at a slightly smaller scale. The decoy lacked the realism of oil stains and tire skid marks seen on all real runways. The decoy buildings, like most decoys, were significantly lacking in activity. They were too clean, without tracks and without the clutter typical of a well-used building complex.

In October 1942 the camouflage project was nearly completed (photo 7-11). From overhead it was already one of the best I have ever seen. The real runway is hard to see on photography, even when you know where to look. Shadows from some of the factory buildings still needed to be eliminated, but the building roofs were well broken up. The decoy factory was still too clean, though landscaping and some 'clutter' was starting to show up. The fake runway showed patches and tonal changes that tended to make it more believable. Fake aeroplanes had been added to help the illusion. Over in the real parking area, real planes were emerging from the factory painted olive-drab so they no longer gave the scene away.

The biggest weakness in this camouflage project was that it did not consider the factory surroundings. Pre-war Japanese intelligence could

173

7-5 Another shot of the Douglas hangar roof. Fake buildings were complete with landscaping and fences. Sheets of light coloured cloth simulated a street.

7-6 Douglas plant roof, 21 October 1942. Detail of fake trees, and showing the posts and guy-wires holding up the fake houses and landscape.

7-7 A wood and canvas car on a muslin street, next to a 2-by-4 and cloth tree on the Douglas plant roof. Attention was given to the shadow the fakes would cast.

7-8 Douglas plant roof with the hangar in the background. Wood, chicken wire, and cloth camouflage was kept open where factory ventilators had to stay in operation.

have easily established (from readily available gas station road maps) that the runway lined up in a specific relationship with the unique 'Ess' curve of the bordering road. While the factory was being so energetically disguised, that characteristic road alignment should have been altered. Either the road next to the factory should have been straightened, or the road at the decoy given the same curve. Even better, both road modifications would have materially enhanced this project.

Compare the aerial photos in the series starting with May when the camouflage had just begun. Using the relationship with the road, it is easy to identify the line of the runway, even on the October imagery when the camouflage was nearly completed. The runway nearly intersected the road at a point slightly to the factory side of the centre of that characteristic reverse curve. A well-briefed Japanese bomb-aimer could probably have found the factory and runway by this simple trick of using the road. The decoy installation might have distracted a few bombers, more at night than during the day, but in all likelihood the factory would not have escaped damage.

This marvellously elaborate camouflage construction was in every respect a creation of Hollywood. It could not have existed in Germany or England. The first heavy rain and/or snow would have ruined it, causing parts to warp or collapse, thus giving away the whole. For all of that it is fascinating to see the art of the movie industry applied like this.

We will never know for sure just how good this work was – the Douglas Aircraft factory camouflage was never put to the test.

7-4 *A barrage balloon hangs over the camouflaged arch of a hangar roof. Bogus buildings had windows and complex roof lines to add to their realism. Douglas plant, 31 October 1942.*

A City Centre

One of the most well known and ambitious camouflage projects of World War II occurred at Hamburg in Germany and was tested often by raiding bombers. The project involved disguising the Binnen Alster and Aussen Alster – two large basins in the centre of Hamburg's business district (photo 7-12). The two basins were created by the damming of the Alster River about a mile short of its junction with the Elbe. Both basins and the Lombards rail and road bridge that divided them were easily recognisable landmarks that identified the heart of Hamburg (photo 7-13).

The Elbe River separated the commercial and residential areas on the north side from the docks, refineries, shipyards and oil storage areas on the south. The well known Alster basins were on a line perpendicular to the Elbe. Between the inner basin and the Elbe was the old section of Hamburg. That characteristic relationship of basins and river was a bomb-aimer's delight. If it could be identified, all Hamburg's targets could be readily located.

When World War II began, the Germans were not concerned with an enemy locating targets in Hamburg.[7] By 1941 the RAF had made it clear

that Hamburg would be visited often.[8] The camouflaging of Hamburg was a signal that the pace and direction of the war were changing. Extensive camouflage at Hamburg dated from that recognition.

The obvious need to make bombing of the city more difficult was equalled by the monumental problems in disguising the two Alster basins. Locks near the Alster mouth protected the basins from the six foot tidal rise in the Elbe. That simplified the camouflage problem some, but there was nothing simple about the rest of the task. Most perplexing

---

7. Hamburg was the third largest city in Nazi Germany (after Berlin and Vienna). It was also the largest port on the European continent and fourth largest in the world. It comprised 288 square miles and had 97 miles of dockage and anchorage space. The battleship *Bismarck* and 45 per cent of German submarines were built here. Hamburg was certainly a prime target.

8. Hamburg was subjected to air raids throughout the war starting with 78 in 1940, 38 in 1941, and 10 in 1942. American bombers joined the RAF over Hamburg in July 1943. There were only 19 raids on the city that year, but each involved hundreds of aircraft. Hamburg was bombed 46 times in 1944 and 49 times in 1945.

was the sheer size of the area to be hidden. The smaller basin (Binnen Alster) alone measured 500 yards (450m) by 450 yards (410m) – a considerable expanse to cover with camouflage, let alone an expanse over open water. In addition, Hamburg averaged between 20 and 30 inches (50 & 75cm) of snowfall each winter, making use of lightweight netting impractical. To compound the problem further, tall smoke stacks, large oil storage tanks and unique patterns of railways, quays and wharves had to be masked or the Alster basin camouflage effort would be for naught.

As with most complex problems, the solution was a complex mixture of camouflage techniques. Large or characteristic buildings were disguised by paint, planting grass and trees on roofs and also the extensive use of nets. Oil storage tanks, originally silver or white to reflect heat, were painted in irregular patterns of dark green and black and covered with netting. Hiding the dock areas became mainly a matter of smoke screens. Bogus road patterns were painted on buildings and across rail lines. Railway tracks themselves were toned down in some places and highlighted in others in an attempt to disrupt the patterns well known to the RAF and British Intelligence from pre-war maps (photo 7-14). The critical elements, the two basins, were camouflaged with sturdy wood and cane frameworks covered by painted cloth mesh and netting.

German camouflage strategy was simplicity itself.[9] Relationships between major elements within the city could not be ignored – they had to appear normal. The Germans rightly assumed that the two large basins would be a bomber's key. British bombers came at night, so the camouflage had to be just good enough to deceive a bomb-aimer working in the poor light of flares or a low moon and looking down through searchlights and flak bursts. Covering the basins would just lead to some other easily recognisable element of Hamburg becoming the reference point. Since the Alster basins had to be present – they had be 'repositioned'. By covering the Binnen Alster right up to the Lombards Bridge and building a 'new' Lombards Bridge in the Aussen Alster, all bomb aiming calculations were thrown off 1,500 feet to the north.

Even the inner basin had to be navigable for large barges, so when pilings were driven to hold a blanketing framework, space was left as a channel. The open run of the channel angled across the Binnen Alster from the river lock to the Lombards Bridge.

---

9. Another German passive defence measure against night bombers, particularly early in the war, was blinding glare from large numbers of 60 and 80-inch searchlights. Dispersed throughout a target area, the glare from these lights made it difficult for bombardiers to pick out their objectives.

7-9 View of the Douglas plant roof from the control tower on the hangar. Scale can be judged from the men on the catwalk (left arrow). Aircraft just completed in the plant are in the right background (right arrow).

7-10 Aerial view of the Douglas plant, 19 September 1942. The decoy runway (far left) was nearly done, but looked too clean. Construction was well along on the decoy factory. The real runway looked like a subdivision and the real factory roofs were nicely disguised. Note the barrage balloons with their circular concrete pads. Silver C-47 transport aircraft appearing on urban streets break the spell.

7-11 Camouflage was nearly completed at the Douglas plant on 2 October 1942. The decoy installation looks reasonable and the actual factory and runway look like part of the city. Finished aircraft were being painted olive drab to make them harder to see. However, relating the runway with the curve of the road in photo 7-2 allows you to see the runway and factory in this photo.

7-12 Hamburg's inner and outer basins separated by the Lombards Bridge. The city centre is in the foreground. Pre-war photo.

Parts of the Binnen Alster camouflage framework were as high as 20 feet (7m) above the water to let small boats pass underneath. Other sections of the inner basin camouflage were simply painted canvas on barges or rafts. As a concession to the weight of snowfall, a metal mesh was used as a grid for the painted cloth covering.[10] Pilings were used as the basis for a fake Lombards Bridge. The decoy bridge was well done in terms of shape and relationship to the relocated dummy Alster basins. Problems with the bridge were that its approaches led nowhere, and it was too clean and uncluttered. The ultimate problem with the whole Alster camouflage project was that British reconnaissance aircraft had been photographing the entire process.

Hamburg's elaborate camouflage was completed before the disastrous 'fire storm' bombings of July and August 1943.[11] Most of the camouflage was burned in that fire (photos 7-14 and 7-16). Photographs taken weeks after the fires show no indication that the camouflage was being rebuilt (photo 7-17). Prior to the fire storm, factories, dwellings and camouflage were all being vigorously rebuilt as fast as they were damaged. After the heavy raids and destruction, Hamburg lost much of its resilience. Nine months later the city had only revived to 88 per cent of its 1943 level of industrial productivity.[12]

What camouflage was left was removed from the Binnen Alster by 1944 because it got in the way of fireboats. The decoy Lombards Bridge was left to deteriorate (photo 7-18). By the end of the war little was left of the Alster camouflage project (photo 7-19).

This camouflage did not save Hamburg from extensive destruction. Probably nothing could have saved the city with the full weight of Allied air power directed against it in massive raids. However, before it was destroyed, the Alster camouflage was apparently effective in protecting some critical targets. Clusters of craters around the ends of the fake Lombards Bridge attest to its utility in drawing bombs away from the real bridge. Ironically, the 1,500 foot (450m) offset of this massive camouflage project was well inside the bombing accuracy of contemporary RAF night strikes. An off-set of three to five miles would have been needed to draw bombs from targets in the city – and given the overall situation of the city and rivers, that would have been impossible to attain.

Doomed from the first by being too large, over water, and being watched during construction, the Hamburg camouflage demonstrated the desperation of local authorities. All of that said, the

---

10. The grid was made of soft iron wire, roughly 18 gauge, woven into a 6-inch mesh. Garnish materials were rags or tufts of natural vegetation, such as coarse grass, attached to the mesh at 6 to 9-inch intervals.

11. Referred to by the Germans as 'the catastrophe' the raids of 24 July to 3 August 1943 accounted for 71 per cent of all the damage done in Hamburg during the war. A total 2,765 Allied heavy bombers dropped 5,125 tons of ordnance in nine separate attacks.

12. Hamburg's population had dropped from a pre-war 1.6 million to 800,000 in August 1943. The city was so badly damaged by the July-August raids that it got only sporadic and light bombing (eight raids) until 18 June 1944.

7-13 Pre-war photo of the Lombards road and rail bridge, Binnen Alster, and the heart of Hamburg. The Alster River exits the Binnen Alster on the left. The Elbe River is in the background.

7-14 Hamburg's camouflage project caught under construction by RAF photoreconnaissance, 8 April 1941. The upper three arrows show paintwork designed to disguise railway patterns. Arrows at lower right show the decoy Lombards Bridge and covered-over Binnen Alster. This camouflage was designed to deceive night raiders.

7-15 Two weeks after the huge RAF and US Eighth Air Force fire bomb raids, much of the Hamburg camouflage had been burned or collapsed. The effect of the fake Lombards Bridge was ruined. The arrow shows the Dammtor Railway Station (see photo 5-15). RAF photo, 18 August 1943.

7-16 Enlargement of photo 7-15 shows the grid construction of the decoy Lombards Bridge and destroyed camouflage in the Binnen Alster. Bare walls show on a number of burned-out buildings.

7-17 Three weeks after photo 7-15, and five weeks after the big fire raids, the Hamburg camouflage still showed no signs of reconstruction. RAF photo, 7 September 1943.

7-18 A strike photo taken during a US raid on 18 June 1944 showed traces of the decoy Lombards Bridge, but the Binnen Alster camouflage was gone. The smoke trails were marker bombs to show where a bomb-bay load was going. The billowing smoke was from fires caused by earlier attackers.

7-19 A 9 April 1945 US photo of Hamburg showing fires started in the dockyards during a 22-plane raid of 4 April 1945. Camouflage was gone from the Alster basins.

Hamburg camouflage stands as an unusually broad area project with a sound concept that was well thought out and well executed in appropriate detail.

An Aeronautical Research Facility

Five miles outside Braunschweig in Germany, the Luftwaffe operated one of the best equipped aeronautical research establishments in the world (photo 7-20). The Luftfahrtforschungsanstalt Hermann Göring had been built at a cost of RM 4 million, and it had been built in secret with concealment in mind (photo 7-21). Because the Allies did not know its location and because its camouflage was so good, and camouflage discipline so careful, the Hermann Göring Research Establishment was never bombed. Nearby Braunschweig was heavily bombed, but the secret facilities were only endangered by two bombs intended for other targets falling wide. Towards the end of the war, Allied fighter-bombers strafed the airfield associated with the research facility. Several hangars and some aircraft were destroyed but the research buildings were neither touched nor suspected (photo 7-22).

Allied photo interpreters never found these facilities, though they had plenty of coverage of the Braunschweig area. This record of survival ranks the Hermann Göring installation with the very best camouflage efforts.[13]

In spite of its two-and-a-half square miles of area and over 100 buildings, the research facility remained covert because of its careful design and a pragmatic approach to its camouflage (photo 7-23).

An airfield was essential, and from the beginning there was no attempt to hide the landing ground. Tourists or spies before the war would have seen planes taking off or landing and reported the location of a 'secret' airfield. This would have just called attention to the facility. Nor was it expected that any camouflage of a landing ground would stand up over the long run.

It was decided to allow the airfield to be overt – to offer a completely normal, but minor facility to mask the real thing. Thus a few hangars and meagre airport facilities were constructed on the side of the grass landing ground nearest a neighbouring village. The strategy was to let the much better equipped Braunschweig airfield a few miles away, attract all the attention. Apparently Allied intelligence was not suspicious that the seemingly normal 'minor airfield' had a landing area half again the size of the civil field serving the city.

Buildings in the Hermann Göring complex were concealed by appearing unobtrusive and widely dispersed. Some were constructed to look like farm buildings and others were built in stands of dense

13. Allied photo interpreters had at least six photo coverages of the Hermann Göring facility between 6 July 1944 and the German surrender in May 1945 but they didn't know it. The photos were small scale imagery, hardly conducive to finding an exceptionally well camouflaged installation. The point is that normal photoreconnaissance was collected in the area without difficulty. Had the secret facility been suspected, large-scale imagery could have been collected easily, facilitating identification.

7-20 Braunschweig, Germany, 25 April 1945. Hidden on this photo is the Luftwaffe's Top Secret Hermann Göring Aeronautical Research Facility. Can you find it? (see Appendix II for the solution.)

183

7-21 *The Luftfahrtforschungsanstalt Hermann Göring, 20 June 1945. The near woods hid aircraft engine research facilities. Normal airfield facilities show out in the open on the right. Flight research hangars, labs, and administrative buildings were in the woods at the upper left.*

7-22 *Overt hangars and at least three airplanes were destroyed by US fighter-bombers, but the real target – the covert installation – remained unseen and untouched. These woods concealed jet engine research stands, a centrifuge to test weapons, a static flight test hangar, and a remarkable high altitude weapons firing tunnel. US photo, 20 June 1945. (see Appendix II for the solution.)*

7-23 *The Hermann Göring centre's weapons test area seen from another angle, 20 June 1945.*

pine forest adjacent to the landing ground. Structures in the forest were purposely built low to let tree cover close over them. Roads were kept narrow and unpaved to preclude aerial recognition of unusual activity.

There were few flaws in this camouflage. Even when you know where to look, few of the 70 major buildings can be seen. During the war, 1,200 people worked at the Hermann Göring facility devising and testing the guns, projectiles and engines that would eventually be used to shoot down the Allied bombers flying blithely overhead.

Contained within the research facility were specialised structures for testing piston and jet engines, wind tunnels for Mach 1.8 and Mach 4 weapons and airframe testing, a ten 'G' centrifuge, machine shops and a host of support buildings. These buildings were made of brick and tile and were not painted nor altered in appearance during the war. They were naturally dull in colouring, but they depended upon the thick tree growth around them for camouflage from horizontal, oblique or vertical observation.

The most remarkable construction and the best camouflage was on a pair of high altitude test firing tunnels. The smaller of the two was designed to simulate guns firing in a cross-wind, such as from a bomber's waist guns. The larger firing tunnel tested projectiles, machine-guns and cannon to be used in Luftwaffe fighters. This underground range was 25 feet (7.6m) in diameter and 1,440 feet (440m) long. Powerful motors in the 'farm' buildings drove multi-stage turbines to suck air from the firing point and tunnel. This installation could be lowered to 0·02 atmospheres, the equivalent of firing conditions at very high altitudes. The large air ducts required for this partial vacuum were disguised by a small building. When the range was in operation, the roof of the building slid to one side leaving the walls of the structure as the mouth of the duct. Properly in place, the duct door was impossible to tell from a normal roof (photo 7-22).

The Hermann Göring installation was large in area but quite limited in actual things to camouflage. It realistically accepted the impossibility of hiding the airfield and elaborately and cleverly hid things like the turbine vents. What actual camouflage there was was well done and thorough. There must also have been outstanding discipline to avoid creating paths and roads into the woods that would have attracted attention to the camouflaged area.

The primary camouflage lessons of the Hermann Göring facility are that: it must be built and disguised in secret; it should take maximum advantage of natural means of concealment; passive defences, no matter how good, are successful over time only if the enemy does not know the camouflaged installation exists. Had Allied intelligence technicians suspected a covert facility in this area, they would probably have found it. The effort to find such a facility would have required resources and risks out of all proportion to having the information – but it could have been done.

What Does it all Mean

Really marvellous camouflage illusions could be devised and artfully constructed, though they always looked better from the ground than from the air. Tactical equipment and positions, large factories, bodies of water, even airfields could be camouflaged for a period of time. What worked against an aircrew with seconds to see the camouflage seldom worked long when frozen by the glass eye.

Photo Interpreters could usually quickly sniff out a fake by a lack of activity or clutter, no height to things that should have three dimensions, or nearby equipment that 'didn't belong'. Little could be hidden from aerial intelligence for any length of time. Time was the key. Given time, repetitive photo coverage, correlation of other intelligence sources, and competent, imaginative PIs, it was a rare camouflage job that remained successful.

Another major problem for camoufleurs on the ground was that intelligence also had the advantage of being able to see the camouflaged area in a broader geographic context. If the deception work did not blend with its environment or just ended, if shadows were not taken into consideration, if lines of communication suddenly disappeared, if seasonal changes were not provided for, the camouflage actually called attention to a place.

Of all the different types of camouflage, tactical camouflage always worked best. First, it was small in scale. Second, camouflage discipline was limited and in the control of people with a vested interest in doing a good job. An individual soldier, vehicle, gun or parked aircraft might be rendered invisible almost indefinitely, but tactical camouflage worked best when its importance was so transitory that the wheels of Intelligence could not grind out identifications fast enough. What that time lapse was depended upon how good the camouflage was and how often the subject area was observed or photographed.

Strategic camouflage – fixed targets – worked only when Intelligence didn't know the target existed. That meant hiding a target from the full spectrum of intelligence collection from the start of construction. Tough to do. The existence and location of an installation could be given away by pre-war travellers, spies, electronic emissions, references in intercepted messages, or prisoner interrogations as well as through aerial photography. Once an important installation was suspected in an area, aerial imagery would be directed against it and its days became numbered. In the long-term it was almost impossible to fool the glass eye.

7-24 *Enlargement of the weapons test area. The roof of the 'farm' building on the left slid back to expose the duct for powerful fans that created low pressure conditions to simulate firing at very high altitudes. The firing range extended underground from the duct to a point 480 yards (440m) to the right, nearly to the static test hangar nestling in the woods at right foreground.*

Appendix 1

Typical Backgrounds

The following photos and captions are from a World War II report on how camouflage should blend into a local background. These were some of the backgrounds British troops expected to encounter.

NORTH WEST AFRICAN BACKGROUND

1. Vineyards on the plain - 100% efficient cultivation makes this artificial pattern; note where it is disturbed by the natural line of the stream. This is difficult country for concealment but stores, tents, etc disposed in straight lines will be less conspicuous than if they are unevenly dispersed.

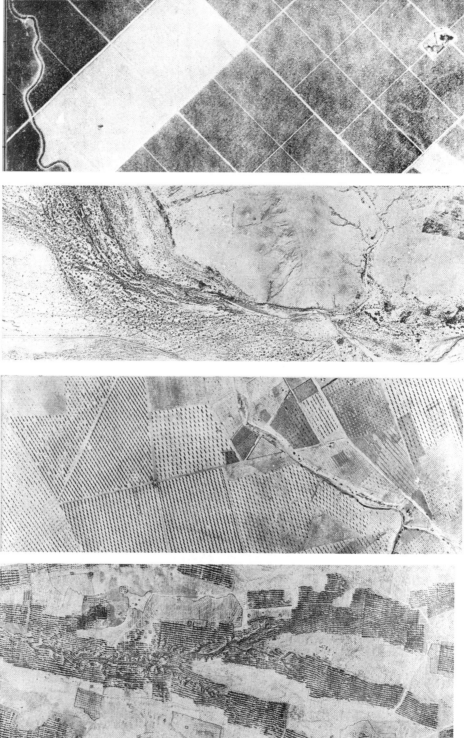

2. Uneven dispersal and desert methods are needed here; every effort should be made to avoid creating formal patterns.

3. Olive grove country in Tunisia. Some cover is available but the background calls for regularity in the dispersal plan.

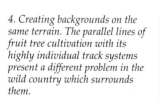

4. Creating backgrounds on the same terrain. The parallel lines of fruit tree cultivation with its highly individual track systems present a different problem in the wild country which surrounds them.

NORTH WEST AFRICAN BACKGROUND

5. Bare mountainous country, where the changing shadows make the chances of concealment vary with the position of the sun.

6. The suburban pattern with its monotonous repetition is common to all countries, but the building unit varies. This is Suburbia as encountered in Tunisia. This pattern will absorb a regular lay-out if suitably adapted.

SOUTHERN EUROPEAN BACKGROUND

1. Fairly wild country but the cultivation pattern is more elastic.

2. A section of suburban pattern is visible here. Compare to picture number 6.

Appendix 2

Photo Solutions

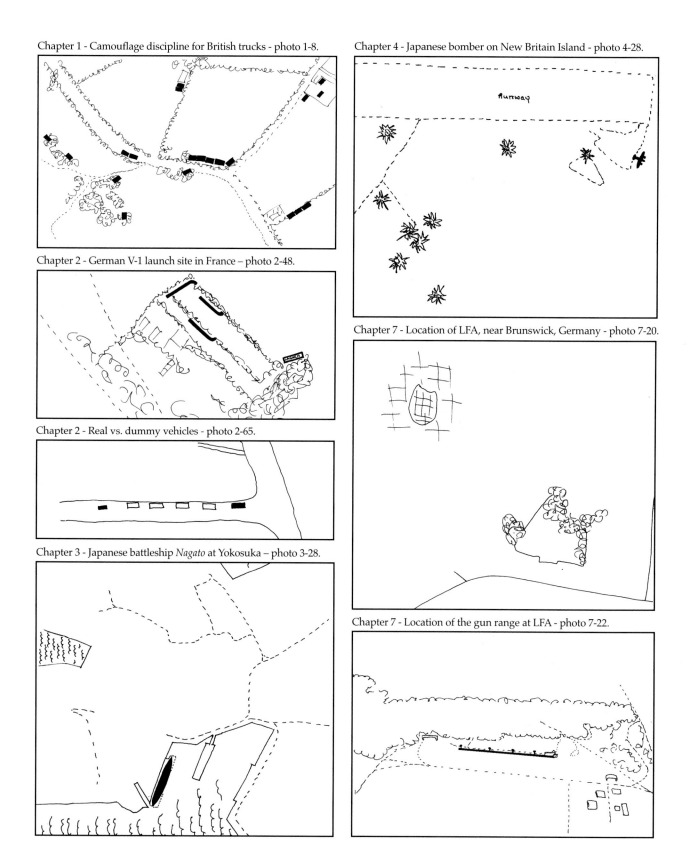

Chapter 1 - Camouflage discipline for British trucks - photo 1-8.

Chapter 2 - German V-1 launch site in France – photo 2-48.

Chapter 2 - Real vs. dummy vehicles - photo 2-65.

Chapter 3 - Japanese battleship *Nagato* at Yokosuka – photo 3-28.

Chapter 4 - Japanese bomber on New Britain Island - photo 4-28.

Chapter 7 - Location of LFA, near Brunswick, Germany - photo 7-20.

Chapter 7 - Location of the gun range at LFA - photo 7-22.

BIBLIOGRAPHY

Babbington-Smith, Constance. *Air Spy.* New York, N.Y.: Ballantine Books, 1957.

Barkas, Geoffrey. *The Camouflage Story.* London: Cassell and Company Ltd., 1952.

Bell, Dana. *Air Force Colours 1926-1942.* Carrollton, TX.: Squadron/Signal Publications, Inc., 1979.

Air Force Colours 1942-1945. Carrollton, TX.: Squadron/Signal Publications, Inc., 1980.

Bowyer, Charles. *Encyclopedia of British Military Aircraft.* London: Bison Books, Ltd., 1982.

Breckenridge, Robert P. *Modern Camouflage.* New York: Farrar & Rinehart, Inc., 1942.

Camouflage,
US Army Training Film TF1–3351, 1943.
A cartoon attributed to the Disney organization.

Camouflage for Aircraft on the Ground. Camouflage Memorandum 129. Fort Belvoir, Va.: The Engineer Board, 1942.

Chesney, Clement H. R. *The Art of Camouflage.* London: Robert Hale Limited, 1941.

Cruickshank, Charles. *Deception in World War II.* New York: Oxford University Press, 1980.

Dewar, Col. Michael. *The Art of Deception in Warfare.* New York, N.Y.: Sterling Publishing Co. Inc., 1989.

Hartcup, Guy. *Camouflage.* New York: Charles Scribner's Sons, 1980.

Industrial Camouflage Manual. New York: Reinhold Publishing Corporation in co-operation with the Pratt Institute, 1942.

Jane's Fighting Ships. New York, N.Y., Macmillan Co., issues for 1941, 1942, 1943 and 1944.

Leyson, Burr W., Capt. *The Army Engineers in Review.* New York: E.P. Dutton & Co., Inc., 1943.

Reit, Seymour. *Masquerade.* New York: Hawthorn Books, Inc., 1978.

Root, Ralph R. *Camouflage with Planting.* Chicago: Ralph Fletcher Seymour, 1942.

Simon, Leslie E., Maj.-Gen. *Secret Weapons of the Third Reich.* Old Greenwich, Conn.: WE, Inc., Publishers, 1971.

Solane, Eric. *Camouflage Simplified.* New York: The Devin-Adair Company, 1942.

Solomon, Solomon J. *Strategic Camouflage.* London: John Murray, 1920.

Stanley, Roy M. II, Col. *Prelude to Pearl Harbor.* New York: Charles Scribner's Sons, 1982.

World War II Photo Intelligence. New York: Charles Scribner's Sons, 1981.

Webster, Sir Charles and Frankland, Noble. *The Strategic Air Offensive Against Germany 1939-1945* (four volumes). London: Her Majesty's Stationery Office, 1961.

Wood, Tony & Gunston, Bill. *Hitler's Luftwaffe.* London: Salamander Books, Ltd., 1978.

Volumes of the United States Strategic Bombing Survey

A Detailed Study of the Effects of Area Bombing on Hamburg.

Bombing Accuracy, USAF Heavy and Medium Bombers in the ETO.

Description of RAF Bombing.

Evaluation of Photographic Intelligence in the Japanese Homeland. Part 5: Camouflage, Concealment, and deception.

Hamburg Field Report.

Huls Synthetic Rubber Plant.

Physical Damage Report, Chemische Werke — Huls Synthetic Rubber Plant.

Physical Damage Division Report (ETO).

The Effect of Strategic Bombing on German Transportation.

Index